Joint Conference of the Boards of Control

Minutes of the Proceedings of the Joint Conference

composed of the boards of control of the World's Columbian exposition

Joint Conference of the Boards of Control

Minutes of the Proceedings of the Joint Conference
composed of the boards of control of the World's Columbian exposition

ISBN/EAN: 9783337848781

Printed in Europe, USA, Canada, Australia, Japan

Cover: Foto ©Andreas Hilbeck / pixelio.de

More available books at **www.hansebooks.com**

Minutes of the Proceedings

OF THE

JOINT CONFERENCE

COMPOSED OF THE

BOARDS OF CONTROL OF THE WORLD'S COLUMBIAN COMMISSION
AND OF THE WORLD'S COLUMBIAN EXPOSITION, WITH
THE REPRESENTATIVES OF THE WORLD'S FAIR
STATE AND TERRITORIAL BOARDS

HELD IN THE CITY OF CHICAGO
December 9th, 10th and 11th, 1891,

Including reports and questions from the Representatives of State World's
Fair Boards, with answers to said questions by Director-
General George R. Davis.

CHICAGO:
RAND, McNALLY & COMPANY.
1892.

Minutes of the Proceedings

OF THE

Conference of the Representatives

OF

STATE BOARDS AND BOARD OF REFERENCE

AND CONTROL.

CHICAGO, DECEMBER 9, 1891.

The Joint Conference, composed of the Boards of Control of the World's Columbian Commission and of the World's Columbian Exposition, together with the representatives of the various World's Fair State and Territorial Boards, met in the Directors' Hall of the World's Columbian Exposition, in the Rand-McNally Building, in the City of Chicago, at 12 o'clock noon, this date, pursuant to a call previously issued for said conference.

President Thos. W. Palmer, of the World's Columbian Commission, in the chair.

Secretary Jno. T. Dickinson, of the World's Columbian Commission, acting as Secretary.

The conference was called to order by President Palmer.

Secretary Dickinson then read the following copy of the invitation to attend this conference, which had been forwarded to the Secretaries of the World's Fair State and Territorial Boards, thus far organized, and to the governors of those States and Territories where World's Fair Boards have not yet been created:

4

OFFICE OF THE SECRETARY,
WORLD'S COLUMBIAN COMMISSION,
CHICAGO, ILL., NOV. 12, 1891.

DEAR SIR: By direction of Hon. Thos. W. Palmer, President of the World's Columbian Commission, I have the honor to extend to your Board an invitation to send a representative to be present and participate in a general conference with the Board of Reference and Control of the National Commission and the World's Columbian Exposition, to be held at World's Fair Headquarters (Rand-McNally Building), in this city, at 12 o'clock noon, Wednesday, December 9, 1891, in accordance with the following resolution adopted by the Board of Reference and Control of the National Commission, October 20, 1891.

Resolved, That the President of this Board be, and he is hereby, authorized and directed to communicate by letter with the several World's Fair boards, where the same shall have been duly constituted by statute, in the several States and Territories; and, in those States and Territories where there are no such Boards constituted by law, with such voluntary organizations as may have been organized by the citizens thereof for World's Fair work, inviting and requesting that a representative from each State and Territory, of such Board or State organization, be present and participate in a general conference with this Board and with the Directory of the World's Columbian Exposition, to be held at the Rand-McNally Building, in the City of Chicago, on the second Wednesday in December, 1891, at 12 o'clock, for the purpose of considering, devising, and formulating such rules and regulations as will most efficiently secure, in the several States and Territories, the systematic coöperation of the State Boards or other organizations in securing proper lines of exhibits, and generally promoting the best interests and success of the World's Columbian Exposition.

Mrs. Potter Palmer, President of the National Board of Lady Managers, especially desires that all ladies who are members of the State Boards also accept the above invitation and be present in Chicago at the time above indicated, in order that they may become fully acquainted with the plans for promoting the work of women, in connection with the World's Fair, in the various States and Territories.

The expense attending the sending of representatives to this conference, it is expected, will be defrayed by your Board.

Trusting that you will, at your earliest convenience, inform me of the acceptance of this invitation, and the name and post-office address of the representatives who will be present on that occasion.

I have the honor to be,

Very truly yours,

(Signed)   Jno. T. Dickinson.

Secretary.

The roll was called, and the following representatives, from the several States named, were present :

Arkansas, Miss J. M. W. Loughborough; California, T. H. Thompson; Colorado, O. C. French, Mrs. Susan R. Ashley; Delaware, Wm. R. Allaband; Florida, W. D. Chipley; Illinois, J. P. Reynolds, Mrs. Frances W. Shepard, Mrs. Frances B. Phillips, Mrs. Richard J. Oglesby, Mrs. Marcia L. Gould, Mrs. Frank Gilbert, Mrs. Robt. H. Wiles, Mrs. James W. Patton, Miss Mary Callahan; Indiana, Clem Studebaker, Mrs. May Wright Sewell, B. F. Havens; Iowa, J. O. Crosby; Kentucky, Mrs. Nancy H. Banks; Maine, Charles P. Mattocks; Massachusetts, Jno. W. Corcoran, E. C. Hovey; Michigan, Isaac M. Weston, Mark W. Stevens, Jas. W. Flynn, E. H. Belden; Minnesota, M. B. Harrison, L. P. Hunt; Missouri, Nathan Frank, Mrs. Patti Moore; Montana, S. De Wolfe; Nebraska, R. R. Greer, A. L. Strang; New Hampshire, Geo. F. Page, E. M. Shaw; New Jersey, S. J. Meeker, W. S. Lenox; North Dakota, H. C. Southard, H. P. Rucker; Ohio, Mrs. Mary A. Hart; Pennsylvania, Arthur B. Farquhar, Miss Mary E. McCandless; Rhode Island, Jno. C. Wyman, Mrs. Amey M. Starkweather; South Dakota, Oliver Gibbs, Jr., Mrs. Jas. R. Wilson, Robt. B. Fisk, Chas. E. Baker; Tennessee, O. P. Temple, J. B. Heiskell; Texas, Jno. T. Dick-

inson; Vermont, A. F. Walker; Washington, Percy W. Rochester; Wisconsin, C. W. Graves, R. B. Kirkland, Mrs. John Winans;
Wyoming, Geo. East; New Mexico, W. F. Thornton.

President Palmer stated that the following resolutions had
just been adopted by the Board of Reference and Control of the
World's Columbian Commission:

Resolved, That the President and members of the Board of
Lady Managers of the World's Columbian Commission, together
with the women representatives of the various World's Fair
State and Territorial Boards now in this city, be and they are
hereby, most cordially invited to attend this conference during
its sessions in this city, and to participate as members thereof in
its deliberations and proceedings.

Resolved, That the Director-General, the Department Chiefs,
and the Chief of Construction be, and they are hereby, invited to
attend the sessions of this joint conference, for the purpose of
furnishing such information to the members of the conference
as may be desired.

Resolved, That any members of the World's Columbian Commission now in this city, and the Directors of the World's
Columbian Exposition, and all representatives of State Boards,
be, and they are hereby, invited to attend the sessions of this
joint conference.

On motion of Commissioner Martindale, the foregoing resolutions were unanimously adopted by the conference.

President Palmer then appointed a committee, composed of
Messrs. Martindale and Flynn, to inform Mrs. President Palmer,
and the members of the National Board of Lady Managers and
women representatives of World's Fair State Boards, that they
were invited to be present and participate in the conference.

Whereupon Mrs. Palmer and the women representatives,
above mentioned, were escorted to the Hall by the committee
and given seats in the conference.

Mrs. Palmer presiding at the conference with President Palmer.

THE PRESIDENT: I have invited Mrs. Potter Palmer to say a few words, but with that delicacy which is one of her characteristics, she refrains. I had then to fall back on Mr. W. T. Baker, the President of the World's Columbian Exposition, who will welcome you, and also probably advance a few ideas that may aid you in formulating your ideas for to-morrow's report. Gentlemen of the convention, I introduce to you, now, Mr. W. T. Baker. [Applause.]

MR. BAKER: Mr. President, what I see before me to-day in the intelligent faces of these delegates more than justifies the expectation that your and our directory indulged in two months ago, when this conference was projected. The value of this conference, if it shall attain the objects that were then had in view, will depend almost entirely upon the intelligence of the members of the State Boards. The object of this conference has been to see if means can not be devised by which the different State Boards, from Maine to California, made if necessary or if possible an integral part of the Exposition, with authority within their jurisdictions to do what may be done for the benefit of the great Exposition as a whole. I have been aware, and I think everybody connected with the Exposition has been aware, for a long time, of the difficulties that will appear some day in managing the business, with exhibitors a thousand or two thousand miles away from us, through our own departments here. It has seemed to us possible to so enlist the coöperation of the different State Boards that they will do that work and do it heartily and intelligently. In order that they may do this work, of course it is essential that they should have the authority to do it from the Board of Control, which will meet here to-day or to-morrow. I believe that the efficiency and the value of the State Boards will rest almost entirely in the outcome of this conference, if it shall be decided by you delegates that you are willing to accept the responsibility which the Board of Control will, I believe, be willing to confer upon you; you will go back to your several States with a mission to perform that will, I think, not only interest you, but will awake the enthusiasm of every State in the country.

Now there are, as I have stated at the outset, some embarrassments that are likely to come to us in the future if we do not have your co-operation in the way of securing exhibits in the first place; and secondly, in the way of discriminating as to what exhibits are worthy to become a feature in the great Exposition. So far as we have progressed, it appears to us that we are rather in danger, as General Walker stated to me a week or two ago, of our own success; that is, in being flooded with more exhibits than we could take care of, or than would be worthy of a place in the Exposition, than otherwise. Now the matter of discrimination must begin at home. If an exhibitor in California has something that he thinks ought to appear in the Exposition, it will have to pass under the judgment of some person some time or other. At the present time that authority rests, here in Chicago, with the departments and with the Director-General. The question is when that department or the Director-General is going to begin to exercise the discretion that belongs to him in discriminating as to what should come here from this long distance. It would be a great injustice to the man in California or Maine or Florida to invite him to come here with, perhaps, some bulky exhibit, and tell him when he arrives here that his exhibit is not worthy of a place in the great Exposition; and so some means ought to be determined to veto that in its incipiency. I believe that there is intelligence enough in the State Boards to accomplish that, and to accomplish it there, with the least friction and the least expense.

There is another view of it that is equally important. I know, and you all know, that there are some few localities still remaining where there is a degree of apathy in regard to the Exposition. In these places the sentiment of the people can not be aroused in any better manner than by you yourselves—these very State Boards. You know everybody in the State that ought to exhibit, and you can see to it that they do exhibit; you can do it a great deal more efficiently than we can do it here; you can do it so that it will be not only to the credit of the great Exposition itself, but to the honor of the State that you represent.

There is another thing. It is known that in previous exhibitions, a great many applications were made for space that was never occupied. Now there is no person at these headquarters that is able to determine definitely the integrity or the good faith of a man, who makes an application for space, a thousand or two thousand miles away; but you can determine that in your own State, and you can know whether the application for space is bona fide, and whether the applicant, if the space is awarded him, will come and occupy it and do it in a fit manner.

These are some of the thoughts that have been in our minds in calling this conference. It is necessary of course that each State that is willing to coöperate in this way should signify it, because we have no power and no authority to enforce obedience to regulations that shall be made here; and then we must agree also upon what the regulations shall be. The regulations, I may say, have to be made by the Board of Control of the Commission. I have nothing whatever to do with it in my official capacity and in what I am saying here now. I am speaking only as one who is interested in the success of the Exposition, and not because I am likely to have any voice whatever in the actual determination of the methods that may be pursued. I have no doubt, however, that the Board of Control will be very glad to have your coöperation, and that they will make such needful regulations as you will agree to, giving you such authority as you will be willing to act under, and so on the whole we shall make this what we have always intended it should be—a National Exposition.

Gentlemen and ladies, I am very glad to welcome you here, and I am more than glad to see the increasing interest in this great work that has almost taken possession of the lives of us who are in it day by day. Before you leave here, I shall hope to have the pleasure of taking you into Jackson Park to show you what has been done by the corporation of which I am an officer. In going there, I shall be glad to make my time yours, and let you suit your own convenience as to when you may go; and if you will determine that for yourselves, I shall be very glad to hear from you sometime, I presume after to-day. [Applause.]

Commissioner De Young offered the following resolution :

Resolved, That when this conference adjourns to-day, it adjourn to meet at half past 10 o'clock to-morrow morning.

Resolved further, That the men and women representatives of the various World's Fair State Boards present at this conference be, and they are hereby, requested to prepare reports setting forth the form of World's Fair organizations in their respective States, amount of appropriation made, work thus far accomplished, and any other matters that they may regard of sufficient importance to be embodied therein, and that they also be requested to prepare, with their report, but separate therefrom, a list of such questions as they may desire answered by the officers of the Commission and Exposition, to the end that the said representatives may receive all the information regarding the World's Columbian Exposition that it is in the power of the management to furnish.

Resolved further, That in order to expedite the consideration of these reports and queries, the Secretary shall, immediately upon the convening of the conference to-morrow morning, proceed to call the roll of States ; and as each State is called, the representatives thereof shall submit their reports and lists of questions, which shall be immediately read, considered, and acted upon, and this method of procedure shall be continued until the reports of all representatives present have been received and disposed of.

The foregoing resolutions were adopted.

Mr. Graves, of Wisconsin, offered the following resolution:

Resolved, That it is the sense of this conference that all applications for space, from exhibitors residing in the United States, be made to the several State Boards direct, and by them forwarded to the Director-General; and that the allotment of space to individuals or corporate exhibitors be finally awarded without the approval of the State Board of the State from which such application was filed.

On motion of Mr. Graves, the foregoing resolution was laid over for action by the conference at its session to-morrow.

Mr. Frank, of Missouri, offered the following resolution:

Resolved, That the representatives from the various State Boards form an organization at the conference to-morrow, to the end that such organization may project a harmonious system to carry out the purposes of their creation, and with the view of aiding the World's Columbian Exposition and the World's Columbian Commission in their work.

Mr. Frank amended the foregoing resolution, so that it be considered at the present time instead of to-morrow; and finally, on motion of Mr. Frank, the resolution was laid on the table for consideration by the conference at to-morrow's session.

Mr. De Young moved that when the conference adjourns to-day, to meet at 10 o'clock to-morrow morning, that it adjourn to meet in the Council Chamber of the City Hall, which had been tendered to Secretary Dickinson by Mayor Washburne for this purpose.

After some discussion, Mr. De Young withdrew this resolution, and on motion of Mr. Chipley, of Florida, the conference passed a vote of thanks to Mayor Washburne for his courtesy in tendering the use of the Council Chamber.

Mr. Chipley, of Florida, called the attention of the conference to the rules and regulations for the government of State exhibits, which had been adopted both by the World's Columbian Commission and the World's Columbian Exposition, on May 1, 1891, particularly directing attention to Article Sixth of these rules, and especially to the three exceptions in Article Sixth; the entire article, with the exceptions, reading as follows:

Sixth. Such State buildings shall be maintained as a State or Territorial headquarters, under the control of the State Board, but subject to the rules and regulations governing the Exposition, for the convenience and entertainment of residents of the particular State or Territory, and the reception and en tertainment of their friends and such guests as they may invite to share the hospitality of such State or Territory; and shall also, if desired by the State or Territory, be used as a depository for a collective exhibit of such a line as shall best illustrate and exemplify the natural resources of such State, as well as its historical and archæological features. Each such collective State exhibit shall, however, be installed and maintained only subject to the following conditions, limitations, and restrictions, to-wit:

 · (*a*) These exhibits shall not be catalogued, nor considered as competitive, or at all entitled to participate in prizes or awards, nor be within the jurisdiction of the committees or juries of award.

(*b*) They shall embrace no manufactures, goods, or products.

(*c*) No processes shall be included therein, and no motive power permitted in any such building.

This article was discussed at considerable length, although it was understood that it would come up for consideration at to-morrow's session, under the resolution of Commissioner De Young requesting the representatives present at the conference to submit in writing such questions as they desired answered by the officers of the Commission and the Exposition.

Without taking any action in regard to this matter, and after having heard Commissioners Martindale, Massey, and De Young, and Director-General Davis on the subject of the rules and regulations governing State exhibits, the conference then adjourned to meet in the Directors' Hall at half past 10 o'clock to-morrow morning.

Just prior to adjournment a note was read, from Miss Kate Field, inviting the members of the conference to attend a meeting in behalf of free art, in connection with the World's Fair, at the Athenæum Building, at 4 o'clock this afternoon.

CHICAGO, DECEMBER 10, 1891.

The conference, composed of the Boards of Control of the World's Columbian Commission and of the World's Columbian Exposition, together with the representatives of the various World's Fair State and Territorial Boards, met in the Directors' Hall of the World's Columbian Exposition, in the Rand-McNally Building, in the City of Chicago, at 10.30 o'clock A. M., this date.

President Thos. W. Palmer, of the World's Columbian Commission, in the chair.

Secretary Jno. T. Dickinson, of the World's Columbian Commission, acting as Secretary.

The roll was called, and the following representatives, from the several States named, were present:

Arkansas, Miss J. M. W. Loughborough; California, T. H. Thompson; Colorado, O. C. French, Susan R. Ashley; Delaware, Wm. R. Allaband, Henry C. Conrad; Florida, W. D. Chipley; Illinois, John P. Reynolds, Mrs. Frances W. Shepard, Mrs. Frances B. Phillips, Mrs. Richard J. Oglesby, Mrs. Marcia L. Gould, Mrs. Frank Gilbert, Mrs. R. H. Wiles, Mrs. James W.

14

Patton, Miss Mary Callahan; Indiana, Clem Studebaker, B. F.
Havens, Mrs. May Wright Sewell; Iowa, J. O. Crosby, H. W.
Seaman; Kansas, A. S. Johnson; Kentucky, Charles P. Mattocks,
Mrs. Nancy H. Banks; Massachusetts, E. C. Hovey, Jno. W.
Corcoran; Michigan, Isaac M. Weston, Mark W. Stevens, Jas.
W. Flynn, E. H. Belden; Minnesota, M. B. Harrison, L. P. Hunt,
Mrs. Frances B. Clark; Missouri, Nathan Frank, Mrs. Patti
Moore; Montana, S. De Wolfe; Nebraska, R. R. Greer, A. L.
Strang; New Hampshire, Geo. F. Page, E. M. Shaw; New Jer-
sey, S. J. Meeker, W. S. Lenox; North Dakota, H. C. Southard,
H. P. Rucker; Ohio, Miss Mary A. Hart; Pennsylvania, Arthur
B. Farquhar, Miss Mary E. McCandless; Rhode Island, Jno. C.
Wyman, Mrs. Amey M. Starkweather; South Dakota, Oliver
Gibbs, Jr., Robt. B. Fisk, Chas. E. Baker, Mrs. Jno. R. Wilson;
Tennessee, O. P. Temple, J. B. Heiskell; Texas, Jno. T. Dick-
inson; Vermont, A. F. Walker; Washington, Percy W. Roches-
ter; West Virginia, W. N. Chancellor; Wisconsin, C. W. Graves,
R. B. Kirkland, Mrs. John Winans; Wyoming, Geo. East; New
Mexico, W. F. Thornton.

Of the Board of Reference and Control there were present,
besides Hon. Thos. W. Palmer, presiding, Commissioners Geo.
V. Massey, M. H. de Young, William Lindsay, J. W. St. Clair,
and E. B. Martindale; and of the World's Columbian Exposition, President William T. Baker; and on behalf of the National
Board of Lady Managers, Mrs. President Palmer.

The minutes of yesterday's meeting were read and approved.

In compliance with the resolution offered by Commissioner
de Young at yesterday's session and adopted, the President
stated that reports, in accordance with said resolution, were in
order, and thereupon the roll by States was called, and the fol-

lowing named representatives read and presented written reports, which were received and filed; but previous to the calling of the roll and reading of the various reports, it was agreed, on motion of Mr. Graves, that any questions accompanying the reports should be taken up and discussed after all the reports had been read.

Arkansas, Miss J. M. W. Loughborough; California, T. H. Thompson; Colorado, Mrs. Susan R. Ashley; Delaware, Henry C. Conrad; Florida, W. D. Chipley; Illinois, John P. Reynolds, Mrs. Frances B. Phillips; Indiana, B. F. Havens, Mrs. May Wright Sewell; Iowa, J. O. Crosby; Kentucky, Mrs. Nancy H. Banks; Maine, Charles P. Mattocks; Massachusetts, Jno. W. Corcoran; Minnesota, L. P. Hunt; Missouri, Nathan Frank; Montana, S. DeWolfe; Nebraska, R. R. Greer; New Hampshire, Geo. F. Page; New Jersey, S. J. Meeker; North Dakota, H. C. Southard; Ohio, Miss Mary A. Hart; Pennsylvania, Arthur B. Farquhar, Miss Mary E. McCandless; Rhode Island, Jno. C. Wyman; South Dakota, Oliver Gibbs, Jr.; Tennessee, O. P. Temple; Texas, John T. Dickinson; Vermont, A. F. Walker; Washington, Percy W. Rochester; West Virginia, W. N. Chancellor; Wisconsin, C. W. Graves; New Mexico, W. F. Thornton.

Mr. Johnson, of Kansas, asked leave to make his report at to-morrow's session, which was granted.

Mr. O. C. French, of Colorado, and Mr. Isaac M. Weston, of Michigan, made oral reports.

President Baker, of the World's Columbian Exposition, then stated that, in accordance with the understanding had with the representatives at yesterday's session, for those who desired to go on a tour of inspection to Jackson Park to-day, he had made special arrangements for transportation, and that the Illinois

Central train would leave the Van Buren street station at
2:30 P. M.

Mr. Chipley moved that President Baker's invitation be
accepted for 9:20 o'clock A. M., to-morrow, the 11th instant.

The motion was lost.

On motion of Mr. Crosby, President Baker's invitation was
accepted for 2:30 o'clock to-day.

On motion of Mr. Graves, it was agreed that when the conference adjourns to-day, it adjourn to meet to-morrow morning
at 10 o'clock.

By request, Mrs. Potter Palmer, President of the National
Board of Lady Managers of the World's Columbian Commission,
then addressed the conference upon the creation, organization,
and work of the Board of Lady Managers.

Mrs. Palmer addressed the conference as follows:

MR. PRESIDENT, LADIES AND GENTLEMEN OF THE CONVEN-
TION: — Knowing the value of the time of this convention, I shall
state as briefly as possible the purposes of the Board of Lady
Managers. The organization of the Board was authorized by the
Act of Congress which created the World's Columbian Commission, section six of which reads as follows: "And said Commission
is authorized and required to appoint a Board of Lady Managers,
of such number and to perform such duties as may be prescribed
by said Commission. Said Board may appoint one or more
members of all committees authorized to award prizes for
exhibits, which may be produced in whole or in part by female
labor."

Thus, after providing for a Commission to take charge of the
Columbian Exposition, Congress at the same time authorized
the organization of a Board of Lady Managers, not certainly,
because the Commission was not equal to the performance of the
task assigned it, nor with the intention of giving women any
undue advantage. It could have only been a practicable

acknowledgment of the really helpless position of industrial women, and of the fact that they and their work might be overlooked and neglected, and probably would be, in the coming Exposition.

As the legislation, capital, and largely the business sagacity and experience of the country, are in the hands of men, it would seem that the voteless ones should have some friends to stand as sentinels, with power to protect their interests.

The further privilege given by Congress to the Board, that of appointing jurors to pass upon the work of women, is a still stronger indication of the intention of Congress that women should not suffer injustice, but be insured fair and impartial treatment.

I must state, however, that our province is not simply to care for the interests of women. At the time of our first meeting, in November, 1890, one of the first powers or duties given us by the Commission was that of working side by side with the men in the various States to promote general interest in the Fair and the work to be shown at the time of the exhibition. We consider that we have a double function: while we must, in a special way, look after the interests of women, we at the same time are just as much interested as is the Commission in the general work being carried on in every State and Territory of this country, and I am sure that the representatives from the various States here, will say that that has been the attitude of the women of each State.

In November, 1890, the Board of Lady Managers met and organized. After its adjournment, the first work assigned its members was to provide for the appointment of women on the various State Boards, as without such recognition in every State and Territory, and a share of the appropriations made in each instance, the work of the Board would have been rendered very difficult.

In the bill sent out by the Director General as a suggestion to the legislators in the various States to assist them in preparing World's Fair bills, the important clause providing for the
2

appointment of women on the State Boards was most unfortunately overlooked. This vital fact having been discovered by the Board of Lady Managers, another bill was immediately printed at their instigation, and sent to the members of the legislatures and to the Lady Managers of the various States and Territories. The reports, as they came from the different States last winter, showed that our members were doing valiant service in the preliminary work of seeking to have women appointed on the Boards of their respective States, and of procuring the needed appropriations. We were gratified to learn that the legislatures in many States had the Exposition first brought to their attention for official action by the members of our Board, and that much of the enthusiasm aroused, both in legislatures and conventions held in the interests of the Fair, was created by our members and their friends, whose appeals to State pride were energetic, well-timed, and eminently successful. The amended bill by which women were given representation on the State Boards and a share of the funds to carry out their work, was thus, through the efforts of the Board of Lady Managers, generally adopted, and was based upon their representation of the work to be done for women in each State.

The standing of the Board having been fully established by the legislation of the various States and Territories, and by the subsequent action of Congress, the Commission, during its meeting in April, 1891, passed the following resolution:

WHEREAS, The Act of Congress, approved March 4, 1891, explicitly recognizes said Board of Lady Managers and provides that $36,000 of the appropriation made for the use of the World's Columbian Commission for the fiscal year ending June 30, 1892, shall be used for the said Board of Lady Managers; now, therefore, for the purpose of more fully fixing and defining the powers and duties of said Board of Lady Managers;

Resolved by this Commission—First. That the Board of Lady Managers be, and they are hereby, directed and empowered to appoint one or more members of all committees authorized to award prizes for exhibits which may be produced in whole or in part by female labor; and the number of such women members so to be appointed shall be in proportion to the percentage of female labor performed in the production of such exhibits.

Second. That the said Board shall have the management and control of the building known as the Woman's Building.

Third. That said Board shall have general charge and management of all the interests of women in connection with the Exposition; and it is hereby recognized and declared to be the official channel of communication through which all women or organizations of women may be brought into relation with the Exposition, and through which all applications for space shall be made for the exclusive use of women or their exhibits in the buildings, or for the construction of buildings intended exclusively for women's use in the Exposition; and that in respect to these and all similar matters, connected with the preparation for, and the management of the Exposition, in so far as the same relates to women's work, women's exhibits, and women's interests in general, the direction and approval of the Board of Lady Managers, through its President, shall be necessary before final and conclusive action is taken.

The various powers conferred upon the Board by Congress, Commission, the Directory, and the legislature of most of the States and Territories, influenced the Board to decide to mark the first participation of women in an important national enterprise by gathering, in the competitive exhibit in the general buildings, such a representation of women's work and of all statistics and data in connection therewith as will show progress made by women in every country in the world during the century in which educational and other privileges have been granted them, and also the increased usefulness that has resulted from the enlargement of her opportunities.

The Board of Lady Managers has, therefore, invited the women of all countries to participate in this great exhibit of women's work, so that it may be made, not only national, but universal, and that all may profit by a free comparison of methods, agencies, and results. The Board regards it of first importance that such a representative collection be secured as will give an adequate idea of the extent and value of the work being done by women in the arts, sciences, and industries. It will also attempt to show the bread-winners who are fighting, unaided, the battle of life, the new avenues of employment that are constantly being opened to them, and in which of these their work will be of the most distinct value, by reason of their adaptability, sensitive and artistic temperaments, and individual tastes; what education will best enable them to enjoy the wider opportunities awaiting them and make their work of the greatest worth, not only to themselves, but to the world. I regret to have to say that our idea, which we hoped to be the first to carry out, has appealed so strongly to the quick perception of the French that they have, since the public announcement of our plans, seized the idea, and they are already preparing an exhibit of women's work and progress in the past and present, which will be shown in the Palais de l'Industrie next summer, in advance of our exhibits. We are sorry not to have been the first to carry out the exhibit idea, which originated with us; but we feel that it is a great compliment to have the significance of it appreciated by such a people as the French, and we have no question that we can learn valuable lessons from the exhibit that they will prepare.

The Board has decided that at the coming Exposition it will not attempt to separate the exhibit of women's work from that of men, for the reason that as women are working side by side with men in all the factories of the world, it would be practically impossible, in most cases, to divide the finished result of their combined work; nor would women be satisfied with prizes unless they were awarded without distinction as to sex, and as the result of fair competition with the best work shown. They are striving for excellence and desire recognition only for demonstrated merit. In order, however, that the enormous amount of work being done by women may be appreciated, a tabulated statement will be procured and shown with every exhibit, stating the proportion of woman's work that enters into it. The application blanks now being sent out to manufacturers contain this inquiry.

The Board of Lady Managers has been granted, by Act of

Congress, the great and unusual privilege of appointing members of each jury to award prizes for articles into which woman's work enters. The number of women on each jury will be proportionate to the amount of work done by women in the corresponding department of classification. The statement as to the amount of their work will therefore be of double significance, for in addition to the impressive showing of how large a proportion of the heavy labor of the world is being performed by the weaker sex, it will also determine the amount of jury representation to which the Board is entitled.

Beside the extensive exhibit in the general Exposition buildings, women will have another opportunity of displaying work of superior excellence in a very advantageous way in the Woman's Building, over which the Board of Lady Managers will exercise complete control. In its central gallery it is intended to have grouped the most brilliant achievements of women from every country and in every line of work. Exhibits will be admitted only by invitation, which will be considered the equivalent of a prize. No sentimental sympathy for women will cause the admission of second-rate objects, for the highest standard of excellence is to be strictly maintained. Commissions of women, organized in all countries as auxiliaries to the Board of Lady Managers, will be asked to recommend objects of superior merit produced by women, and producers of such successful work will be invited to place specimens in the gallery of the Woman's Building.

Not only has woman become an immense although generally unrecognized factor in the industrial world, but, hers being essentially the arts of peace and progress, her best work is shown in the numberless charitable, reformatory, educational, and other beneficient institutions which she has had the courage and ideality to establish for the alleviation of suffering, for the correction of many forms of social injustice and neglect, and for the reformation of long-established wrongs. These institutions exert a strong and steady influence for good; an influence which tends to decrease vice, to make useful citizens of the helpless or depraved, to elevate the standard of morality, and to increase the sum of human happiness; thus most effectively supplementing the best efforts and furthering the highest aims of all government.

All organizations of women must be impressed with the necessity of making an effective showing of the noble work which each is carrying on. We especially desire to have represented, in the rooms reserved for that purpose in the Woman's Building, the educational work originated or carried on by women from the Kindergarten organizations up to the highest branches of education, including all schools of applied science and art, such as training schools for nurses, manual training, industrial art and cooking schools, domestic economy, sanitation, etc. When not practically exhibited, the work of all such organizations should be shown by maps, charts, photographs, relief models, etc., but it is earnestly hoped that one at least, the most representative institution in each of these branches, will be shown from every State and every country, in order that a comparison may be made of the systems.

Commissions co-operating with the Board of Lady Managers will be asked to aid them:

1st. To procure a representative exhibit showing the work of women in all the varied occupations in which they engage.

2d. To procure as far as possible statistics as to the amount of woman's work that enters into every exhibit, and other interesting data connected with the same.

3d. To recommend to the Board work by women, of such supreme excellence as to be worthy of admission to the gallery of the Woman's Building.

4th. To recommend to the Board, women who have the requisite expert knowledge to serve on various juries of award.

5th. To see that the Educational work being carried on by women, from the primary to the highest branches of education, is exhibited when possible; and when not possible, that it be illustrated by means of maps, charts, photographs, etc.

6th. To see that the charitable and philanthropic work—as well as that to promote recreation, healthfulness, reform, etc.—inaugurated by women is either exhibited or made matter of record, as above.

7th. To aid in giving suitable publicity to the plans of the Board of Lady Managers in all the leading papers, through the agency of Press women, when possible.

8th. To aid in collection of a loan exhibit of old 'ace, embroideries, fans, etc.

9th. To secure the books written by women for the Woman's Library, especially such as relate to the exact sciences, philosophy, art, etc.

Our plans are being developed day by day, and we undoubtedly shall have many more lines of work than those now laid down; but at present these are the plans which we submit for work in this country and abroad. [Applause.]

Upon the conclusion of Mrs. Palmer's address, on motion of Mr. Chipley, the conference expressed its appreciation of, and thanks for, the address by a rising vote, which was unanimous.

Commissioner De Young offered the following resolution:

Resolved, That it is the sense of the convention of the representatives of the boards of the various States of this Union that the Government of the United States be requested, in commemoration of the Columbian Exposition and the event it celebrates, to coin 'hrough its mints pieces of the value of fifty cents. This being the probable price of admission, these coins can be used for that purpose and will make valuable souvenirs. The component parts of said coin to be of gold and silver in due ratio. That five million be struck, and they be made legal tenders.

That the Secretary of this meeting be requested to forward this resolution to Congressman Springer,´ of Illinois, with a request that he introduce such a bill and present this resolution to Congress.

Mr. Rochester moved to refer the foregoing resolution to a special committee of three, for report, which motion prevailed, and the President appointed Messrs. Rochester, De Young, and Gibbs as said committee.

Mr. Chipley offered the following resolution, which was adopted:

Resolved, That the Director-General be requested to have the proceedings of this conference, including Mrs. Palmer's address, printed and furnished the representatives of World's Fair State Boards.

The conference then adjourned until 10 o'clock to-morrow morning.

CHICAGO, DECEMBER 11, 1891.

The conference, composed of the Board of Control of the World's Columbian Commission and the World's Columbian Exposition, together with the representatives of the various World's Fair State and Territorial Boards, met in the Directors' Hall of the World's Columbian Exposition, in the Rand-McNally Building, in the City of Chicago, at 10.30 o'clock A. M. this date. President Thomas W. Palmer, of the World's Columbian Commission, in the chair. Secretary Jno. T. Dickinson, of the World's Columbian Commission, acting as Secretary.

The roll was called, and the following representatives from the several States named were present:

Arkansas, Miss J. M. W. Loughborough; Colorado, O. C. French, Mrs. Susan R. Ashley; Delaware, Wm. R. Allaband, Henry C. Conrad, Mrs. Caleb Churchman; Illinois, John P. Reynolds, Mrs. F. B. Phillips, Mrs. F. W. Shepard, Mrs. Richard

J. Oglesby, Mrs. M. L. Gould, Mrs. Frank Gilbert; Mrs. R. H. Miles, Mrs. J. W. Patton, Miss Mary Callahan; Indiana, Clem. Studebaker, B. F. Havens, Mrs. May Wright Sewell; Iowa, J. O. Crosby, H. W. Seaman, Miss Ora E. Miller; Kansas, A. S. Johnson; Kentucky, Mrs. Nancy H. Banks; Maine, Charles P. Mattocks; Massachusetts, E. C. Hovey, Jno. W. Corcoran; Michigan, Isaac Weston, Mark W. Stevens, James W. Flynn. E. H. Belden; Minnesota, M. B. Harrison, L. P. Hunt, Mrs. Frances B. Clark, Mrs. H. F. Brown; Missouri, Nathan Frank, Mrs. Patti Moore; Montana, S. De Wolfe; Nebraska, R. R. Greer, A. L. Strang; New Hampshire, George F. Page, E. M. Shaw; New Jersey, S. J. Meeker, W. S. Lenox; North Dakota, H. C. Southard, H. P. Rucker; Ohio, Mrs. Mary A. Hart, Mrs. P. M. Hartpence; Pennsylvania, Arthur B. Farquhar, Miss Mary E. McCandless; Rhode Island, Jno. C. Wyman, Mrs. Amey M. Starkweather; South Dakota, Oliver Gibbs, Jr., Robt. B. Fisk, Chas. E. Baker; Tennessee, O. P. Temple, J. B. Heiskell; Texas, Jno. T. Dickinson; Vermont, A. F. Walker; Washington, Percy W. Rochester; West Virginia, W. N. Chancellor; Wisconsin, C. W. Graves, R. B. Kirkland, Mrs. Jno. Winans; New Mexico, W. T. Thornton, Richard Mansfield White.

Of the Board of Reference and Control there were present, besides Hon. Thos. W. Palmer presiding, Commissioners Geo. V. Massey, M. H. de Young, William Lindsay, J. W. St. Clair, and E. B. Martindale; and of the World's Columbian Exposition, President Wm. T. Baker; and on behalf of the National Board of Lady Managers, Mrs. President Palmer.

The minutes of yesterday's meeting were read and approved.

A communication from Richard Allen Dawson, Secretary of the National Convention of Colored Men, 1890-91, asking

"the privilege of appearing before the conference and present-
ing a statement of facts as to what has been done by the colored
people," etc., which was received and filed; and, on motion of
Mr. Frank, Mr. Morris was invited to a seat upon the floor of the
conference.

On motion of Mrs. Palmer, Mrs. Fannie B. Williams (colored).
was invited to a seat upon the floor of the conference.

On motion of Mrs. Phillips, Miss Kate Field, now in the city,
was invited to a seat upon the floor of the conference.

Mr. Farquhar offered the following preamble and resolution:

WHEREAS, The Convention of Delegates having in charge the
interests of the States they respectively represent in the World's
Columbian Exposition, having carefully investigated the scope
and plan of said Exposition, and the ways and means provided
for completing the preparations in a manner adequate to the
requirements of a National undertaking, deem it proper to give
public expression of the result of their inquiries, observations,
and conclusions, in the form of the following resolutions:

Resolved, That the World's Columbian Exposition is an enterprise in all respects National and international in its character,
having been authorized and promoted by the Congress of the
United States. The Act of Congress, as a condition precedent
to locating said International Exposition at Chicago, required
the citizens of said city to furnish a satisfactory site and
$10,000,000, this sum being deemed by Congress sufficient to
complete the work of preparation. We find that the citizens of
Chicago have complied fully with the requirements of said Act
of Congress. They have provided an ample and admirable site,
and have furnished more than ten millions of dollars. We find
also that the growth in every department of science, industry, and
art, and the interest manifested by all the nations of the earth in
the proposed Exposition, celebrating an event marking an important epoch in the history of the world—the discovery of America
—renders it absolutely necessary for the Commission having

jurisdiction to enlarge the scope and plan of said Exposition beyond what was originally contemplated, in order that it might fulfill its mission and comport with the true dignity of the nation. In this the National Commission has but complied in a reasonable manner with the obvious demands of the Act of Congress.

We find that the work has proceeded according to the plans provided by the National Commission, that great progress has been made, and no doubt is left in our minds that if those in charge of the enterprise are properly sustained by the general Government, as they deserve to be, the Exposition will in every respect far surpass, in extent and useful influence, any that has been heretofore held.

After having studied with care the scope and plan of the Exposition, the work so far as it has progressed, and the estimates submitted by the Finance Committee, we are satisfied that at least eighteen millions of dollars will be required to fully and properly complete the work of preparation in a manner creditable to the nation.

We affirm without hesitation that the representatives of the people of the United States in Congress, should promptly appropriate five millions of dollars for the completion of this national enterprise projected by them. The advantages of the Exposition are to be reaped by the citizens of the entire United States. The people of Chicago have contributed five millions of dollars, the city five millions of dollars, and it certainly would be reasonable, under the circumstances, for the rest of the country to contribute an additional five millions of dollars, since the advantage to them is beyond calculation.

As said above, this is a national enterprise, and the credit of the country is at stake. If it fails, it will do us incalculable injury ; if successful, incalculable good. The work should be completed in a manner commensurate with the greatness of the nation, and the importance of the event celebrated, or it should never have been attempted.

Representing the several States of the Union, we recommend our constituents to use their influence to secure an appropriation by Congress of five millions of dollars, upon such terms as may seem just and equitable.

At the suggestion of President Palmer, the consideration of the foregoing preamble and resolutions was deferred until the unfinished business of yesterday's session should be disposed of.

The President then called for the reports of States, which had failed to report at yesterday's session, and none responding, questions from representatives, in accordance with a resolution adopted at yesterday's session, were announced to be in order.

Mr. Massey moved that all questions now propounded, and that all questions that may be propounded during this conference, shall be referred to the Director General, who shall answer them at his convenience after conference with his Department Chiefs.

Mr. Graves moved to amend said motion, by making a request that the Director General answer them now.

Mr. Walker moved, as a substitute for Mr. Massey's motion:

That questions before the conference be now read, and that motions now pending be laid on the table until after the reading.

Which motion prevailed.

The questions were then read, and upon the completion of their reading, Mr. Massey offered the following resolution:

Resolved, That the questions submitted and read, and such others as may be presented, be, and they are hereby, referred to the Director General for consideration and reply by letter to the State Board or organization propounding same.

Mr. Rochester moved to amend said resolution by inserting the following: "And that these questions and answers be published in the proceedings of this meeting, and be furnished to every State in the Union."

Mr. Frank offered the following resolution as a substitute for Mr. Rochester's amendment, which was accepted by him:

Resolved, That the proceedings of this conference be printed with all convenient speed; that the answers to questions propounded be printed, and that copies of the printed pamphlet be sent to the State Boards for information.

The resolution of Mr. Massey was adopted.

Mr. Heiskell offered the following:

Resolved, That the questions filed be again read, and that such of them as relate to matters settled and known shall be taken up, answered, and discussed at present.

Mr. Rochester offered the following amendment to said resolution, which was accepted by Mr. Heiskell:

Resolved, That the questions read be immediately referred to the Director General, and that he be requested to make answers to such as he is prepared to answer.

Mr. Graves offered the following as a substitute for the resolution of Mr. Heiskell:

Resolved, That the Director General be invited to this room, if it is convenient for him to come and listen to the reading of the questions, and answer such of them as it may be convenient for him to answer at this time.

Mr. Havens offered the following resolution as a substitute for all of the foregoing resolutions and amendments, and it was adopted:

Resolved, That the questions submitted be referred to the Director General, and that he be requested to make answers to such as he is prepared to answer, at three o'clock this afternoon.

The resolution of Mr. Farquhar offered earlier in the session was now taken up for consideration.

Mr. Haven moved to strike out the word " appropriation " wherever it occurs in the resolution, and insert the word " loan " in lieu thereof, but subsequently was permitted to withdraw said amendment.

Mr. Frank raised the point of order, that the subject matter of Mr. Farquhar's resolution could not be considered by the conference.

The President ruled that the point of order was not well taken.

Upon the motion to adopt Mr. Farquhar's resolution, Mr. Corcoran moved that a vote be taken by the call of States, and it was so agreed.

Upon the call of States, those voting to adopt the resolution of Mr. Farquhar were: Arkansas, Colorado, Delaware, Indiana, Kansas, Maine, Michigan, Minnesota, Montana, New Hampshire, New Jersey, North Dakota, Ohio, Pennsylvania, Texas, Vermont, Washington, West Virginia, Wisconsin, Wyoming, and New Mexico (21). Present and not voting: Iowa, Massachusetts, Missouri, Rhode Island, South Dakota, Tennessee (6). California and Florida were not present at this conference.

On motion of Comissioner St. Clair, the announcement of the result of the vote was deferred.

Mr. Chancellor offered the following preamble and resolution :

WHEREAS, It is the sense of this conference that the active co-operation of the World's Fair Boards of the several States and Territories should be invoked (in so far as it may be legally practicable so to do) in securing proper lines of competitive exhibits from individuals or corporations within their respective States and Territories ; and,

WHEREAS, Under the Act of Congress and the regulations for the allotment of space already prescribed, pursuant to the authority of said Act, it is not believed that this co-operation can be effectively invoked otherwise than as the medium for furnishing reliable information as to the quality and character of the proposed exhibit, as well as the character and standing of the intending exhibitor, and expressing approval or disapproval thereof ; and that while it is understood that applications for the allotment of space may be either forwarded directly, or through the Board of the State or Territory wherein the intending exhibitor resides, to the Director General, it is nevertheless deemed important that the Board of each State or Territory shall be promptly advised of every such application as shall be made directly to the Director General, so as to be enabled to furnish the information desired touching the same, and expressing approval or disapproval thereof ; and this conference, therefore, respectfully suggests and recommends to the Board of Reference and Control of the World's Columbian Commission the adoption of the following resolution :

Resolved, That the Director General shall promptly forward to the Board of the State or Territory whence any such applications shall emanate, copies of all such applications for the allotment of space as shall have been transmitted directly to that officer, and that the several Boards be requested to furnish information to the Director General, in such form and manner as he may prescribe as to every application.

And, upon the adoption of such resolution by the Board of Reference and Control, this conference, as the representative of the several State Boards assembled herein, pledges the hearty and active aid and co-operation of each such State or Territory in this particular line of work, as well as in every other in which its agency can properly be employed for promoting the interest and success of the World's Columbian Exposition, in each of the several Departments thereof.

Mr. Graves called up as unfinished business his resolution offered on the first day of the session :

Resolved, That it is the sense of this conference that all applications for space from exhibitors residing in the United States be made to the several State Boards direct, and by them forwarded to the Director General, and that no allotment of space to individuals or corporate exhibitors be finally awarded without the approval of the State Board of the State from which such application was filed.

Mr. Corcoran offered the following as a substitute for Mr. Chancellor's resolutions:

Resolved, That all applications for the space allotted for exhibitors be referred primarily to the several Boards of State Managers for their consideration and determination, under such rules and regulations as the Board of Control may prescribe ; provided, however, that for cause shown an appeal may be allowed by said Board of Control to any applicant aggrieved by any determination of a Board of State Managers.

On motion of Mr. Frank, the consideration of the foregoing resolutions were temporarily deferred.

After some discussion on the resolutions offered by Mr. Farquhar, the President ordered the announcement of the vote upon the adoption of said resolutions, and it was done, as follows:

    States voting for the resolution.................... 21
    Present and not voting.......................... 6
    Not present at the conference.................... 2

The following named representatives stated in substance that, in their official or representative capacity, they did not feel justified in voting for Mr. Farquhar's resolution; but as individuals were willing to have their names recorded as being favorably disposed to the intent and purposes of the resolution, and their names were thus recorded: Messrs. John W. Corcoran and E. C. Hovey, of Massachusetts; John P. Reynolds, of Illinois; J. O. Crosby, of Iowa; Nathan Frank, of Missouri, and John C. Wyman, of Rhode Island.

Mr. Rochester, from the committee to whom was referred the resolution of Commissioner de Young, reported back said resolution amended, and asked that it be adopted.

Said resolution as amended reads as follows:

Resolved, That it is the sense of this Convention of the representatives of the Boards of the various States of this Union, that the Government of the United States be requested, in commemoration of the World's Columbian Exposition and the event it celebrates, to coin through its mints pieces of the value of fifty cents. That being the probable price of admission, these coins can be used for that purpose, and will make valuable souvenirs. The component parts of said coin to be of *such metal or metals as will give it a distinctive character;* that five millions be struck, and that they be made legal tenders.

That the Secretary of this meeting be requested to forward this resolution to Congressman Springer, of Illinois, with a request that he introduce such a bill and present this resolution to Congress.

On the motion to adopt said resolution, a rising vote was demanded, and the resolution was rejected. Ayes—7; nays—14.

Commissioner White, on behalf of the Lady Manager from Delaware, offered the following resolution, which was adopted:

That a vote of thanks be given to Mr. Baker for the special car, placed at the disposal of this conference, to visit and view the grounds and buildings of the Exposition.

The resolutions of Messrs. Graves, Chancellor, and Corcoran were then taken up.

Mr. French moved to refer said resolutions to a committee of three for a report.

President Baker moved to amend said motion, by making said committee consist of six members, three from the State Representatives and three from members of the Board of Ref-

3

erence and Control, which amendment was accepted; and the
motion, as amended, having been adopted, the President
appointed, as said committee, Messrs. Graves, Chancellor, and
Corcoran, of the Representatives; and Commissioners Lindsay,
Massey, and Martindale, of the Board of Reference and Control.

Mr. Frank called up the following resolution, which had been
offered at the first session of the conference, and subsequently
withdrew it:

Resolved, That the representatives from the various State
Boards form an organization at the conference to-morrow to the
end that such organization may project a harmonious system to
carry out the purposes of their creation, and with the view of
aiding the World's Columbian Commission and the World's Columbian Exposition in their work.

Mrs. May Wright Sewall offered the following resolution,
which was adopted:

Resolved, That it is the sense of this conference that the
interests of the Columbian Exposition will be advanced by the
participation of women with men in every State Commission;
and therefore the conference recommends that in all States
where the organic law does not forbid it, women be placed on
the State Commission; and that where the law does now prevent
this action, that an effort be made to have the law amended; and
further, that in order to secure intelligent harmony between the
plans of the Board of Lady Managers and the State Boards, that
the Lady Managers from each State be included in the State
Commissions.

On motion of Mr. Frank, the conference took a recess until
1.45 P. M.

———

Upon the reassembling of the conference, at 1.45 P. M., President Palmer announced that Mr. Morris, who had been admitted
to a seat in the conference, was present and desired to address the

conference; thereupon, Mr. Morris addressed the conference, and at the conclusion of his remarks offered the following resolution:

Resolved, That a committee of five be appointed from this conference for the purpose of considering the ways and means by which the interest of the Exposition can best be promoted among the colored people throughout the United States, and that said committee formulate and report a plan to this conference, and the same, if adopted, be recommended by this body to the Board of Control for its approval.

The President announced that the resolution would lie upon the table until the regular business should be disposed of.

Commissioner Lindsay, on behalf of the committee to whom had been referred the resolutions of Messrs. Graves, Chancellor, and Corcoran, reported the following resolutions, which were adopted:

WHEREAS, It is the sense of this conference that the active co-operation of the World's Fair Boards of the several States and Territories should be invoked (in so far as it may be legally practicable so to do) in securing proper lines of competitive exhibits from individuals or corporations within their respective States and Territories, it is therefore

Resolved, That the World's Columbian Commission, or its Board of Control, should adopt such regulations as may be necessary to enable such of the said State or Territorial Boards, as may so desire and request, to inquire into and consider the propriety of all exhibits that may be offered by any citizen or resident of their respective States or Territories; and it is the opinion of this conference that such State or Territorial Board should be empowered to receive, and to forward to the Director-General, applications for space, with such recommendations and information as they may deem proper. And it should be provided that in case any proposed exhibitor shall apply directly to the Director-General, the application should be referred to the Board of his State or Territory, and final action thereon deferred until such Board shall have had fair and reasonable opportunity to consider and report upon the same.

Mr. Frank made the following announcement :

Since the morning session, when I withdrew from the consideration of the conference the resolution proposing an organization of the Representatives of the State Boards, sincere regret has been expressed at my so doing. I therefore give notice, that if occasion calls for it, and the request is made of me hereafter by three Representatives so to do, I shall ask the Representatives to meet in Chicago for the purpose of considering and of carrying into effect said resolution.

Director General Davis then appeared before the conference, in compliance with the request contained in the resolution adopted at this morning's session, and spoke in reference to the subject matter originating in said resolution. The questions which had been propounded, he took up and answered *seriatim*.

Mr. Havens offered the following resolution, which was unanimously adopted :

Resolved, That the thanks of the members of the conference be returned to Hon. Thos. W. Palmer, the President thereof, for his prompt, fair, impartial, and courteous treatment of all, as the presiding officer of our meeting.

On motion of Mr. Corcoran; the convention adjourned *sine die*.

Reports of the Representatives

State and Territorial Boards

ARKANSAS.

MR. PRESIDENT, LADIES AND GENTLEMEN:

In making my report of the work thus far accomplished in the State of Arkansas, I desire to say that the bill to appropriate a sum of money toward a representation of the products of the State at the World's Fair, which passed the House of Representatives last winter, failed to pass the Senate, owing to the fact that a two-thirds majority is required for appropriation bills.

This was greatly regretted by all liberal-minded citizens, and a movement was immediately started for raising funds by popular subscription. At the request of many prominent people, Governor Eagle called a World's Fair Convention, which was held in Little Rock, on the 6th of August, at which there were present not less than two representatives from each county.

This convention adopted a charter for a stock company of $100,000, with shares at $2 each, to be known as the Arkansas World's Fair Association, Col. J. H. Clendening, of Fort Smith, being elected President.

This charter provides for a Board of Directors (the number being not yet decided upon), who shall elect a State Board, composed equally of men and women; to the women will be given five per cent. of all funds collected.

Under the leadership of Mrs. Eagle, assisted by Mrs. Edgerton—these ladies being the National Commissioners for the State —the interests of the women will be well represented.

The general interests of the State have been thus far most ably managed by Governor Eagle and our two National Commissioners, Maj. Jno. D. Adams and Col. J. H. Clendening, very influential men.

In the report of the Secretary of the Chamber of Commerce of Fort Smith, of which Colonel Clendening is President, the following statement is made:

Five hundred and twenty letters of inquiry have been received and answered, and more than 600 letters have been sent out through this organization by President Clendening in working up an interest in the two World's Fair Conventions which were held in Little Rock, in January and August of this year.

There will be a meeting of the Arkansas World's Fair Association held in Little Rock to-day, for the purpose of perfecting a plan of permanent organization.

It is to be regretted that the organization could not have been perfected sooner, but the State will soon be in a position to outline its plan of work.

Arkansas was proud to welcome the distinguished President of the Board of Lady Managers, Mrs. Potter Palmer, and the Secretary of the World's Columbian Commission, Colonel Dickinson, who assisted so materially during their recent visit in arousing an interest among the people of our State in the coming Exposition.

With her extensive coal mines, iron, silver, and copper ore, large products of manganese, beautiful native woods, and the fruits which grow to such perfection in the State, Arkansas will have every reason to be proud of her exhibit.

It is to be regretted that two of the most important features of our State can not be exhibited at the World's Fair, as each would lose its efficacy in transportation. The first of these, the wonderful medicinal waters of the Hot Springs; the second, our salubrious climate.

JEAN LOUGHBOROUGH,
Delegate for the State of Arkansas.

CALIFORNIA.

CHICAGO, ILL., December 10, 1891.

HON. THOS. W. PALMER, *President World's Columbian Commission.*

SIR: In compliance with the resolution of yesterday, I would respectfully submit the following report:

The last Legislature of California made an appropriation of the sum of $300,000 for the purpose of erecting a building, collecting and maintaining an exhibit of the products of California at the World's Columbian Exposition, etc. This sum is now available and at the disposal of the Commission appointed by the Government.

As yet no plan for a building has been decided upon, but several architects are at work, and it is expected that we shall be ready to commence the erection of a building as soon as the weather will permit.

Within the past few months, much work has been done throughout the State in personal interviews and correspondence with individuals and exhibitors, and that there will be a good representation from California, in all departments, there is little or no doubt in the minds of the Commission.

And that the exhibit within the State building will be as thoroughly complete of our products and resources as the rules of your honorable body will permit us to make it, there is still less doubt.

The State Commission has also organized County World's Fair Associations in nearly all the counties of the State, and through a large and organized membership of its associations, we hope to keep up the feeling of enthusiasm until we get the State fairly represented inside of Jackson Park.

THOS. H. THOMPSON,
Secretary California World's Fair Commission.

COLORADO.

MR. AND MRS. PRESIDENT, LADIES AND GENTLEMEN:

The General Assembly of the State of Colorado, in creating our State Board of World's Fair Managers, declared as full members the Committee and Alternates, the Lady Managers and Alternates, made the Governor of the State President of the Board, and gave him the appointing of five other members, who should, with himself, equally represent the two leading political parties. We have, therefore, fourteen members on our State Board, four of whom are women.

In dividing the work of the State, in order to handle it more easily while within our own borders, we made but seven classes. The last class named embraces the supervision of women's work throughout the State, in all its branches, both in usual and unusual lines of labor, and this class was placed unreservedly in the hands of the four women of the Board. We had not asked of our Legislature a separate appropriation for the women's work, but when we found that the State Board had been so generous as to give us so large a part of the work to do, and, moreover, had so divided it as to give us a distinct department, we asked the Board to set aside for our use a certain per cent. of the State appropriation. With characteristic generosity, 15 per cent. was placed to our credit.

As you doubtless all know, our Legislature voted us $100,000. But they did more than this; they allowed a clause in the Act which reads: "The Board of County Commissioners of the several counties in this State may make such appropriations as to them may seem proper, not to exceed 2 mills on the dollar on the assessed valuation of the taxable property of the county making such appropriation, for the purpose of enabling them to secure a proper representation of their resources, manufactures, products, and interests at the World's Columbian Exposition of 1893." Of course, the counties have been asked to make an appropriation, and to such as comply has been given the appointing of their own agents to collect exhibits, etc.

In order to secure the appointment of a woman with whom the other women of the Commission would heartily co-operate, we have placed this matter before the ladies of the most populous town in each county of the State, we asked them to consider the work we hope to do, as outlined in a circular letter to them, and together agree upon the lady who, in their opinion, will do them and their county the greatest credit, then ask her appointment of their Commission. As these appeals have been made to every county in the State, even where no appropriation has been made, an enthusiastic interest has been created among the women, and a local pride aroused which, we hope, will lead to a search for worthy exhibits. Excepting this interest, the organizing of clubs for study, in order to fit the members for the better appreciation of the exhibits of the Exposition of 1893, and also for the gathering of information relating to the production or discovery of objects worthy of being sent by our State to the Exposition, we have as yet attempted but one collection; this is the gathering, arranging, and classifying of our native flora, which it is thought is the most varied of that of any State in the Union. It is estimated at upwards of 3,000 varieties. As our State covers so much territory—you may not know that we have four counties nearly as large as the State of Connecticut, nineteen as large as Delaware, and thirty-seven as large as Rhode Island—and as the four women on our Board live in widely separated sections, unless you outline for us a better plan, we will either divide the class of work given us to do into four subdivisions, and each hold herself responsible for one of these divisions of work, or leaving the class as it now stands, as our State is twice as large as Illinois, dividing it into four sections, which will give each one of us quite enough to do, if each but looks after one section.

I believe Mr. French's report covers all the rest of the ground, and although I do not wish to bring up again the vexed question of the rights of State buildings, I would like to know, if those parties who contribute to the decoration of our State building would be allowed to sell within its walls any article, for instance books of native flora, photographs of scenery—provided the State Board was willing to allow this privilege?

SUSAN RILEY ASHLEY,
Denver, Colorado.

COLORADO.

Mr. President:—I desire to supplement Mrs. Ashley's report with a brief statement touching our financial resources, and the manner of organizing for the World's Fair work in Colorado.

To the $100,000 appropriated by the eighth General Assembly of the State has been added $40,000 by county appropriations, which sum, it is confidently believed, will be increased to $50,000 by the counties yet to take action; liberal donations of money and material have been tendered the State Board by corporations and individuals to aid in the construction of the State building they have decided to erect; so that, from all sources, we expect to have in the aggregate $175,000 for World's Fair purposes in Colorado.

The State Board consists of fourteen members and was organized on the 16th of May last. Under the law creating the same, the Governor of the State is made President, the other officers being elected by the Board, and are a Vice-President, Secretary, and a Treasurer; the four officers named above constitute the Executive Committee, with authority to exercise all the powers of the Board when the same is not in session, and must report their proceedings in full to the meetings of the Board, which are held quarterly. The classification adopted divides the work into seven departments, namely: Mines, Mining and Metallurgy, Agriculture, Horticulture, Machinery, Education, Historical, and Woman's Department.

The work of the several departments is placed in charge of a chief selected by the State Board, who will be assisted in the Mining Department by three district superintendents. The State having been divided into three districts, in all departments the chief and superintendents will be assisted by County Agents selected by the County Commissioners of the various counties, and paid from the funds appropriated by them. The entire work will be superintended and directed by the State Board.

It is the purpose of the Colorado Board to make a very full and complete display of the numerous and valuable resources of the State, and they are greatly encouraged in the belief that they will be able to do so by the fact that the citizens representing the various industries are offering the most liberal encouragement by their aid, and preparation of exhibits.

The newspapers of the State display a most generous encouragement by full and free publication of all matters in the interests of the Fair, and the railroads are aiding us materially by giving a mere nominal rate for carrying service.

O. C. French,
Representative Colorado State Board.

DELAWARE.

Chicago, Ill., December 10, 1891.

The representative from Delaware would respectfully report that the Legislature of Delaware, at its session last winter, passed an act creating a World's Fair Board of Managers, consisting of nine persons, three of whom are women and six men.

The organization of the Board and the election of an Executive Commissioner have been duly reported to the Director General, and are on record in his office. Steps were taken early in the summer for the location of the Delaware State Building, a committee from the Board of Managers visiting Chicago in June last, and after consulting with the authorities here, a site was selected. At the same time a plan for the proposed building was submitted to the Bureau of Construction, which, through its suggestions, it was deemed best to modify. Our home architect is now at work on the modified plans and they will be ready in the near future for submission to the Bureau of Construction.

The amount of the State appropriation is $10,000, and it is confidently expected that this sum will be supplemented by a further appropriation by the legislature of 1893, sufficient in amount to warrant a full and creditable exhibit from the State.

The women's work is under the control of a committee composed of the three women who are members of the State Board of Managers, with Mrs. Caleb Churchman, of Wilmington, as chairman.

Mrs. Churchman was invited by the State Board to attend this conference, and she is now present with a view of familiarizing herself with the work in hand, in order that she and her co-laborers may enlist the hearty support of the women of Delaware in the World's Columbian Exposition.

In addition to the regular representative, Messrs. Mathias T. Moore and Henry C. Conrad, two members of the Delaware State Board, are in attendance at this conference.

Respectfully submitted,

W. R. ALLABAND,

Representative.

FLORIDA.

CHICAGO, ILL., December 10, 1891.

HON. THOMAS W. PALMER, *President World's Columbian Commission, Chicago.*

SIR: In compliance with resolution adopted at the conference of yesterday, I submit my report for Florida.

I regret to say that no appropriation was made by the Legislature.

Being forced to rely upon personal efforts of our citizens, a convention was called at Orlando, which convened on the 8th of October. The convention was large and representative, and was presided over by Governor Fleming.

At that convention, a Board of Directory for Florida was appointed, composed of thirteen members. The National Commissioners of Florida, both men and women, were made *ex-officio* members of the State Board. Since its organization four ladies have been added to the Board to assist the National Lady Commissioners.

Under the authority vested in the Board by the State Convention, the directory has moved forward under a plan of voluntary assessments, in their endeavor to raise $100,000, and will continue their efforts, I think, with success; and we hope to make a creditable display of Florida's wonderful resources.

I will mention an offer made by the Board to the children who are regular attendants at any school in the State.

To each scholar who will collect a minimum $100 for the World's Fair fund, the Board issues a certificate agreeing to pay the expenses of the holder from Florida to Chicago and return and six days' board at Chicago and admission to the World's Fair.

The children will go under proper chaperons. The certificate provides for an alternate, but beyond this alternate it is absolutely not transferable. While the Board expect to net some money from this plan, the offer was the outgrowth of a higher motive. Besides interesting their parents, we believe the Fair will be the greatest educator of this generation, and a week's attendance will give the children more practical education than months at school, in addition to a lesson in patriotism.

The children, when they return home, will send many others to see the great Exposition.

Respectfully,

W. D. CHIPLEY,
President Florida's World's Fair Directory.

REPORT FOR THE STATE OF ILLINOIS AT THE CONFERENCE OF STATE COMMISSIONERS WITH THE BOARD OF CONTROL OF THE WORLD'S COLUMBIAN EXPOSITION.

CHICAGO, December 10, 1891.

HON. THOMAS W. PALMER, *President:*

In accordance with the resolution passed by the conference yesterday, requiring the representatives of the State Boards here assembled to report as to the forms of organization and the progress of their labors to date respectively, I have the honor to submit the following for the State of Illinois:

The Illinois Board of World's Fair Commissioners is composed of the present members of the State Board of Agriculture, twenty-one (21) in number.

Its officers consist of a President, Vice-President, Secretary, and Director-in-Chief.

The State Government, in its *municipal capacity*, is itself the only exhibitor, and I can not better or more clearly state the character, scope, and purpose of the proposed exhibit than to quote the organic act on that subject, which provides as follows:

"The said Board of Commissioners is hereby empowered to obtain and cause to be properly installed in said exhibition building or buildings a *collective, departmental exhibit* for the State . of Illinois, which shall illustrate the natural resources of this State, together with the methods employed and results accomplished by the State, in its *municipal capacity*, through its several departments, boards, commissions, bureaus and other agencies, in the work of promoting the moral, educational, and material welfare of its inhabitants, so far as such methods and results are susceptible of exhibition in the manner proposed."

Included by special provision in this collective exhibit are:

First. A model common school-room of high grade, fully equipped and furnished, under the direction of the State Superintendent of Public Instruction.

An illustration of the methods and results of educational work as pursued in the State normal universities, the public, technical, and art schools, and the high schools of the State.

An exhibit by the University of Illinois of the equipment, methods of instruction, and achievements of that institution in its several departments.

An exhibit of the educational and industrial work, as conducted in the State charitable institutions.

An exhibit illustrating the entire system of the inspection of the several varieties of grain, as established by the State Railroad and Warehouse Commission and practiced by the State Grain Inspection Department.

Second. Collections, correctly classified and labeled, illustrating the natural history and archæology of this State, including its stratigraphical and economic geology; its soils, subsoils, useful clays and ores, and other products of mines and quarries; its botany and zoology, with the products of forests, lakes, and rivers; also, an exhibit, by the State Fish Commission, of native and cultivated live fish, with hatchery appliances, equipments for transportation, and models of fishways in use; also, a full and complete collection of all the cultivated products in the several branches of agriculture, farm culture, horticulture, and floriculture, in illustration of the widely different conditions of soil and climate under which rural husbandry is practiced in the various sections of this State.

Third. Architectural drawings (with elevations) of every public building erected and now used or maintained, in whole or in part, by the State, with map showing the location of each, and accompanied by historical and explanatory notes and tables; also maps, charts, diagrams, and tables for the State, and, so far as practicable, for each county, showing its geology, distribution of useful minerals, its topography, with its lakes, rivers, canals, and railways, its climatic conditions, its industrial growth and increase in population by decades, from the date of organization to the year 1890, together with such other physical features as possess a scientific interest or would be taken into account in estimating the ability of our territory to maintain a dense population.

The relation of the departments and agencies of the State to the work of preparation and maintenance of the exhibit is defined specifically as follows :

"It is hereby made the duty of the officers of the several departments, boards, bureaus, and commissions in the service of the Government of this State, to co-operate with the said Board of Commissioners in collecting and arranging for exhibition such material as may be available for display in illustration of the methods employed and results achieved in their respective lines of official duty, and, if so required by said Board of Commissioners, they shall furnish complete catalogues, direct the installation, assume the immediate care while on exhibition, and cause the removal of their respective exhibits at the close of said World's Columbian Exposition, in accordance with the requirements of the management of the same. The said Board of Commissioners is also hereby authorized to accept loans or donations and, with the approval of the Governor, to acquire, by purchase, for the State, specimens and material, if deemed necessary, to supplement any of the said departmental exhibits.

"Consent of the General Assembly is also given that there may be placed on exhibition, as part of said *collective exhibit*, in a suitable fire-proof structure to be erected for the purpose, such relics and trophies belonging to, and in custody of, the State, as the Governor may designate; the same to be and remain at all times, during their removal, while on exhibition, and during their return to their present depository, in the sole care and charge of their official custodian."

The amount appropriated to the Board is $720,000, of which they are instructed to devote the sum of $40,000, to the encouragement of an exhibit of live stock owned in the State of Illinois. Of this sum, the Board is simply the disbursing agent upon whatever basis may seem to itself the most efficient and equitable.

It will be observed that, with a single exception, the work to be performed, the chief agencies to be employed, and the duties to be discharged do not touch or relate to the private personal interest of any individual citizen.

The considerations which served to determine our General Assembly to provide for an exhibit of the character proposed are:

1. The chief significance and practical value of the Columbian Exposition will be found in the opportunity it will afford for comparison of National progress, such comparison necessarily involving a searching inquiry as to the proper forms and functions of government.

2. It was deemed essential to the *completeness* of this important international event that *some* State of the "great republic" should do what is here proposed for Illinois, in illustration of the functions of a government under the republican form guaranteed to every State by our Federal Constitution.

3. By reason of the great honor conferred upon her by the location of the Exposition, the educational and financial benefits which her citizens must reap in greater measure and at less cost than those of any other, the obligation resting upon the State of

Illinois was easily recognized and cheerfully acknowledged by the necessary legislation.

The plans for making the collection have been practically arranged; the work of preparation in the several departments has fairly begun; the apportionment of the funds to the respective sections of the exhibit has been substantially made; the contract for the construction of the State building, with its completion limited to October 10, 1892, has been executed; and if the collective exhibit shall be installed as contemplated, it will present to the observer an illustration of the natural resources and conditions for human life as fixed in permanency upon the territory of Illinois, and also of the methods and achievements of the various agencies in the service of the State Government in promoting the moral, educational, and material welfare of our citizens.

The Illinois Woman's Exposition Board.

In the same Act of the General Assembly which created the Illinois Board of World's Fair Commissioners, provision is made for the organization of the Illinois Woman's Exposition Board—which is also represented in this conference—whose specific duty is to secure the representation of the industries of the women of the State of Illinois at the World's Columbian Exposition.

There is not any legal official connection between these two Boards. Their paths and administrations are radically distinct, as will doubtless appear from their reports to this conference; and I mention the latter only to say that, so far as my information extends, there is a widely entertained opinion among our citizens that the exhibit secured by them should be installed in the State building, and that, in recognition of such opinion, and at their request, one-tenth of the exposition space in that building has been placed at their disposal by unanimous vote of the other Board, subject, of course, to the desired approval of the higher authorities.   Respectfully submitted,

JOHN P. REYNOLDS,
Director-in-Chief,
Illinois Board, World's Fair Commissioners.

4

Gentlemen of the Board of Control:

In responding for the Illinois Woman's Exposition Board, I can not report the work in so advanced a condition as it would please us all to have it. We have, however, been diligently looking over the field, and are gradually maturing plans for the display of the skill and the industries of the women of Illinois, · which we believe will result in a showing creditable to our sex, and which may surprise those who do not know in what a variety of callings women now work and succeed.

Some question has arisen as to our right to exhibit manufactured articles and processes in the Illinois State Building, where space has already been assigned us, and it is desirable that we have such interpretation of the rules made by the Board of Directors of the Fair as shall set all questions of this kind at rest. I therefore improve this occasion to call your attention particularly to this subject.

The work of the Illinois Woman's Exposition Board is to appropriately represent the industries of the women of the State of Illinois at the great Exposition. The ladies composing the Board of which I am the President understand the statute to mean that they are to make a collective display of the industries, skill, and work of the women of the State, and they understand it is for this purpose particularly that the law allows them the $80,000 now at their disposal. We understand further that, in a general way, the entire exhibit from Illinois is under the control of the Board of Illinois World's Fair Commissioners, which Board is provided for, and its duties defined, by the same Act of the Legislature which creates the Illinois Woman's Exposition Board. The law says, this Illinois Board of Commissioners "shall exercise the general management, control, and supervision of all matters pertaining to the grounds, structures, *and exhibits* of the State of Illinois at the World's Columbian Exposition," etc. This Board of Commissioners have accordingly set apart to the Illinois Woman's Exposition Board one-tenth of the space in the large and elegant building which they are constructing, in which space it is intended we shall make a display of woman's industries and work.

Now, we have heard some question has arisen as to whether the rules and regulations of the Board of Directors, or of the Board of Control, will permit us to display the industries and· skill of the women of Illinois in this State building. It is thought by some that such a display in that place will be in conflict with the rule of the Directors which prohibits the exhibition of manufactured articles in a State building. It is sincerely hoped by the members of the Woman's Board of Illinois that no such rigid construction will be put upon the rule referred to, or else that the rule itself may be changed to admit of our displaying the skill, and work, and industry of Illinois women in the manner that it was intended by the law-makers they should be displayed, and in the manner that it is desired by both the Boards of Illinois to have the work done.

I will further say in this connection that it is not the purpose of the Illinois Woman's Board to display manufactured articles strictly *as* manufactured articles. They do, however, desire to make whatever displays may be necessary in order to show the art, the skill, the handicraft, and the industries of the women of this State, and unless they are permitted to do this, it is not apparent how the purpose of the statute, creating the Board, can be carried out, or how the appropriation at the disposal of the Board can be expended, consistently with the chief object in view.

The women of Illinois have done creditable work in dentistry, in pharmacy, in the fine arts, in the learned professions, in sanitary science, and in mercantile and manufacturing pursuits. As physicians, surgeons, and nurses, they now take a prominent place. Women have, in short, done work worthy to be exhibited in most departments of human activity, and the work of woman's hand and brain in its complete state represents, of course, in most cases, what might, in one sense of the term, be called manufactured articles. Yet we can not believe it is intended to exclude manufactured articles in the sense here stated from a place in the

State Building of Illinois. In this State building it is expected and desired that the collective display of the work and industries of Illinois women will be exhibited. It is even seriously questioned by many whether the Illinois Woman's Board has any power or authority to make such a collective display elsewhere than in the State building, and among those who take this view are found the men who were most active in securing the passage of the statute which provides for a woman's display.

Of course I do not mean by this to be understood as saying that exhibits and displays in other appropriate Departments of the Fair by Illinois women are not to be encouraged, or even that they are not to be pecuniarily supported by the Illinois Woman's Board. It is now expected that we shall assist women to exhibit, where we deem the subject of exhibition a proper one, in other places than the collective State exhibit which it is desired shall be located in the Illinois State Building. Passing over, for the present, exhibits of this kind which are to be entered for competition and prizes, I, for the present, deem it important to call the particular attention of this Board to the matter of the Illinois Women's collective display. I voice the sentiment of the entire Board in expressing the hope that we may forthwith have such an understanding in regard to this subject as will enable us to go forward in our work with a certainty that the plans we make will not be thwarted by any rules of this Board or of the Board of Directors, or by any construction that may be put upon the rules now in existence, adopted for the government of the Fair.

FRANCES B. PHILLIPS,
President Illinois Woman's Exposition Board.

INDIANA EXECUTIVE COMMISSIONERS' REPORT.

MR. PRESIDENT, LADIES, AND GENTLEMEN OF THE CONFERENCE: In compliance with the resolution under which we have assembled, I submit the following:

The law creating the Board of World's Fair Managers for Indiana was passed by the Indiana Legislature in March, 1891.

The amount of our appropriation was made, in the sum of $75,000. The Board consists of thirteen Commissioners from each of the two leading political parties, making twenty-six; the Governor, the four National Commissioners and their alternates, the State Geologist, State Statistician, and the President of the State Agricultural Society. The officers are as follows: President, Clem Studebaker, South Bend, Ind.; Vice-President, Charles B. Stuart, LaFayette, Ind.; Secretary, Wm. T. Noble, Indianapolis, Ind.; Treasurer, Frederick J. Hayden, Fort Wayne, Ind.; Executive Commissioner, B. F. Havens, Terre Haute, Ind., making thirty-eight members in all, on our Board. We have a lady member on each committee, and one committee composed wholly of lady members. We have no Board of Lady Managers, exclusively.

The Board was organized in May, 1891, by the election of the four officers first named. At this meeting, the manner of procedure by the Board to make the best exhibit possible at the Exposition, was carefully canvassed, and resulted in creating a system of departments largely similar to those of the World's Columbian Commission.

These departments are as follows: Department A—Agriculture, food and food products, farming machinery and appliances, horticulture, viticulture, and floriculture. Department B—Live stock of every kind and description, including domestic and wild animals, fish and fish culture. Department C—Manufactures and machinery, including electricity and electrical appliances. Department D—State Building and building materials, including forestry and forest produce. Department E—Mines, mining, and metallurgy, including the stone, coal, clay, kaolin, and cement, in raw and manufactured state, and natural gas. Department F—Education, liberal, fine, and decorative arts, and associated charities, including a full display of our common-school system and our public and private benevolent institutions.

These committees have complete and full charge of directing the work in their departments, and are held responsible therefor by the Board.

COMMITTEE ON WOMAN'S WORK.

This committee consists of all the lady members of our Board. They have entire charge of everything relating to women's work, in our State, pertaining to the securing of a creditable exhibit of everything relating to women's work from Indiana.

An Executive Commissioner was elected in September.

The Board from our State commenced work at once. The site for the Indiana Building was promptly secured by Judge Martindale. Plans for a handsome social club-house and reception rooms have been adopted and the contract to build the building will be let February 4, 1892, in which many exhibits illustrative of Indiana's growth in every department will be made under the rules of the World's Columbian Commission. It is expected that this building will cost about $35,000, and it is intended to make the building an elaborate exhibit and display of Indiana's best building material.

Applications for space have been sent to all manufacturing institutions in our State. These applications have been sent out in duplicate, and, when returned, one will be filed with our Board and the other forwarded to the Director General at Chicago for his action thereon.

Our Board has already arranged for Indiana furnishing her quota of natural forest trees, nine in number, with other material to go into the construction of the Forestry Building at the Exposition, and other material for this building.

A concluding and further report will be made from the Committees on Education and Women's Work, by the Chairman of the Committee on Women's Work, Mrs. May Wright Sewall, of Indianapolis.　　　Respectfully submitted,

B. F. HAVENS,
Executive Commissioner.
One of the Committee.

INDIANA WOMAN'S COMMITTEE REPORT.

The Educational Committee is organized under four departments; or rather to it is assigned a fourfold task:

First. It is to collect and arrange for the Exposition such materials as are necessary to show the development of education in our State, through all its grades, from the kindergarten to and including the university. The two lines along which the system has developed, the material and the intellectual, will be kept in view; to show the material, plans and examples of school buildings, appliances, apparatus, and furniture will be shown; while the intellectual growth will be presented by means of charts, tables, and monographs, and by a display of the work actually done at the present time.

Second. This committee is to present the charitable, philanthropic, reformatory, and penal institutions of the State, and the work done by them, through photographs, reports, and monographs.

Third. To show the development of the Fine Arts and of Decorative Art, and the present state of these arts in Indiana, is also assigned to the Committee on Education, which is, moreover, fourth, and finally, charged with preparing an exhibit of the achievements of Indiana in literature and in journalism, and of submitting, with this exhibit, a monograph on the literary development of the State.

This committee has an agent who is a paid officer of the State Commission. The Committee on Education has voluntarily assumed the burden of raising, by subscription, moneys to assist in carrying on its work. The scheme of what is called the " Penny Fund " originated with Mrs. Harrell, a member of the committee. Briefly, the plan is this:

With the approval of the State Superintendent of Public Instruction, all schools in the State have been asked to take up a collection on a certain day, the same day being everywhere observed. It is intended that to this collection every pupil registered in any school in the State shall contribute 1 cent; every teacher, 10 cents; every principal of a school, 25 cents; each superintendent of a system of schools, 50 cents; and every school officer, $1.

The first collection has been taken, and from the returns already received (the date of the collection was the third Friday in November) it is inferred that it will amount to nearly $8,000.

The day set apart for the collection of the Penny Fund is called "Exposition Day," and in order to make the preparation for the collection educational, the committee directed one of its members, Mrs. Sewall, to prepare a programme to be rendered by all the schools of the State on the same date. Out of this will probably develop the celebration in our schools of a series of Exposition Days during the current school year and that of 1892 and 1893. The primary object of these fêtes is to increase the time given to the study of American history in schools of all grades, and to stimulate the sentiment of patriotism among the children and young people. An article setting forth the plan of Exposition Day, and containing materials for programmes, etc., will appear in the December number of the *Journal of Education* of Indiana.

The special committee, called Committee on Women's Work, includes the nine women in our State Commission, viz.: the five directly appointed by the Governor as regular members of our State Commission, and the two members from Indiana on the Board of Lady Managers, with their alternates.

The committee is organized with Chairman and Secretary. The work it has undertaken is to see that the work done by the other committees, the industrial activity of Indiana women, shall obtain full recognition; to ascertain the number of industries in which women in our State are engaged, and the number of women engaged in each; to ascertain the number of women who are proprietors of business enterprises. It is the purpose of this committee to have statistical charts, which will set forth the present industrial and pecuniary condition of the women of our State, hung on the walls of the Indiana Building.

The Woman's Committee, in response to the request of Mrs. Palmer that the women of every State shall make some contribution to the interior finishing or furnishing of the Woman's Building in Jackson Park, have asked the privilege of being charged with one room in that building.

The Women's Committee have also undertaken to take charge of the finishing and furnishing of the apartments in the Indiana State Building, set apart for their use, and our plans include having all the furniture in these rooms made after designs furnished by our women and in great degree made by women.

It is probably considered by the men of our commission that the most important function of our committee is to arouse interest and inspire enthusiasm in the Columbian Exposition. In reaching the people of all localities, our committee will avail itself of the agency of communication furnished by the women's clubs of the State, and by the farmers' and teachers' institutes.

Our circulars of information and circulars of appeal (in general already approved by the commission) are not yet issued, and will not be issued until after the next meeting of the State Commission, which is set for February 4th.

Perhaps the committee considers that one of the most important features of its work is preparing for exhibition the contribution made to the development of our State in philanthropy reform, and social culture, through the organized effort of women.

Respectfully submitted by

MAY WRIGHT SEWALL,
Chairman of Committee on Women's Work,
for the Indiana State Commission.

IOWA.

To Hon. THOMAS W. PALMER, *President of the World's Columbian Commission :*

In response to the resolution of this conference, calling upon the representatives of the respective State Boards of Columbian Commissioners to report the action already taken in World's Fair matters in the States they represent, the undersigned, representing the Iowa Columbian Commission, respectfully submits the following :

The General Assembly of Iowa holds only biennial sessions, and, being about to adjourn, by an Act approved April 15, 1890, entitled "An Act to provide for a creditable exhibit of the resources of the State of Iowa in the Columbian Exposition or the World's Fair, to be held in Chicago," set forth the following preamble :

"WHEREAS, Congress is now considering, and the House of Representatives has already passed, a bill providing for a World's Fair, to be known as the Columbian Exposition, and held at Chicago during 1892 or 1893," and, to be in time, the Act provided for the appointment of an Iowa Columbian Commission of eleven members, one from each congressional district of the State, and appropriated the sum of $50,000. But, in case the Exposition be not held before 1893, not more than 10 per cent. of that sum should be drawn from the State Treasury before the convening of the Twenty-fourth General Assembly, and the remainder covered back into the Treasury ; and the subject of further appropriations should be referred to the next General Assembly, which convenes in January, 1892, leaving only $5,000 available before that time.

Pursuant to this law, the Executive Council of the State appointed eleven Commissioners, who met at the Capitol and organized on the second day of September, 1890.

The following is a corrected list of members and officers of the Iowa Columbian Commission, as at present existing:

First district, Theo. Guelich, Burlington; second district, H. W. Seaman, Clinton; third district, F. N. Chase, Cedar Falls; fourth district, James O. Crosby, Garnavillo; fifth district, S. B. Packard, Marshalltown; sixth district, J. W. Jarnagin, Montezuma; seventh district, Henry Stivers, Des Moines; eighth district, S. H. Mallory, Chariton; ninth district, Charles Ashton, Guthrie Center; tenth district, John F. Duncombe, Fort Dodge; eleventh district, William Hamilton Dent, Le Mars.

Officers and Committees—Vice-President and Acting President, James O. Crosby; Treasurer, William Hamilton Dent; Secretary, F. N. Chase.

Executive Committee—S. H. Mallory, J. W. Jarnagin, John F. Duncombe.

Committee on Rules and Plans—H. W. Seaman, Charles Ashton, James O. Crosby.

Auditing Committee—Henry Stivers, James O. Crosby, S. B. Packard.

President Johnston, member from first district, died at his home in Keokuk, May 17, 1891.

James Wilson, of fifth district, resigned, January, 1891.

The Commission has held six sessions, and adopted rules of order; and, from time to time, has adopted reports of its Committee on Plans for the formation of a State exhibit, as follows:

1. Each member of the Commission was required to ascertain and report the agricultural, industrial, mechanical, educational, and other resources and advantages of the congressional district of his residence, that are worthy of being represented at the Columbian Exposition.

2. That provision be made for assisting all individual exhibitors of the State in the transportation of their exhibits to the Exposition and return, and, upon their arrival, that a competent person shall be in attendance at Chicago, to give full information and assist in seeing to their proper location, according to classification and allotted space.

3. There shall be prepared, under the supervision of the Superintendent of Public Instruction, an Educational exhibit of the State University, State Agricultural College, all colleges and academies, all high schools, all normal schools and State teachers' associations. And there shall be a State map showing the location of each school-house in the State.

4. That statistical charts be prepared of all State institutions, showing their history and extent, with full statements of their management.

5. That Ottumwa be requested to furnish a model of its Coal Palace, Creston of its Grass Palace, Sioux City of its Corn Palace, and Forest City of its Flax Palace.

6. That an exhibit of soils to the depth of five to six inches be prepared to show as it is in place, and to be taken from different counties, so as to fairly show the soil of different localities throughout the State.

7. A geological map, or set of maps, after the model in "White's Report of the Geology of Iowa," vol. 1, page 33. Being a series of maps so constructed and placed, one over the other, that, by cutting out parts, will show at a glance the geological period exposed at the surface throughout the different sections of the State.

8. A collection of specimens illustrating the geology and mineralogy of Iowa, as they occur in place, from the Lower Silurian to the Cretaceous, capped by the upheaval of the Sioux quartzite. To be laid up in relative proportions in twelve wooden cases, 10x12 feet square, six feet high, with glass fronts; each classification to be labeled, and with a statement of its average thickness.

9. That the proprietors of each working quarry of building stone be requested to furnish a sample of his quarry, in form of a twelve-inch cube, with different dress for each face, but one face left to show its clearage.

10. That a collection be made of all the known varieties of grasses in the State, both wild and cultivated, and artistically arranged for an exhibit.

11. That the State Horticultural Society be invited to prepare an exhibit that shall worthily represent the horticultural products of the State.

12. That the State Agricultural Society be invited to prepare a like exhibit of agricultural products.

13. That the State Historical Society be invited to make an exhibit, by means of charts and publications, of the history and growth of the State.

14. That the State Fish Commission be invited to present an exhibit showing the growth of pisciculture in the State.

15. A committee has been appointed to gather complete statistics showing in full the number of periodical publications in the State, the frequency of their publication, and whether political, religious, scientific, or professional, and the circulation of each; and it was resolved that a room be provided exhibiting them all at the Iowa headquarters, with accommodations for the members of the State Press Association.

16. A committee has been appointed to gather statistics of the religious interests of the State, to wit: the names of the religious denominations within the several counties, the number of church buildings and parsonages, and their value, the number of denominational schools, and the value of buildings and endowments, number of students, number of ministers and church members, number of Sabbath schools, officers, teachers, and scholars, volumes in library, etc.

The Secretary was appointed as general promoter of the interests of the Iowa State exhibit among the people of the State, and during the present year has devoted his time almost exclusively to the work.

A small building was erected by the Commission on the grounds of the State Agricultural Fair, for use as headquarters in 1891 and 1892, and during the last September fair was in charge of a committee that distribute a large amount of World's Fair literature of our own publication, as well as that received from the Department of Promotion and Publicity of the National Commission.

Shortly after the proclamation was issued by the President of the United States through the Department of State, our Commission issued an address to the people of the State of Iowa, which was sent to all the newspapers of the State, with a request for its publication, and it was very generally published.

Second only to the State of Illinois, Iowa made application for a site upon which to erect a State building, and a location was assigned to her on the 13th of February, 1891, by the Committee on Grounds and Buildings.

H. W. Seaman, Esq., was appointed to advertise for plans of State Buildings, and nine competitive plans were presented, induced by the announcement that, upon the selection of one by the Commission, its author would be chosen upon the usual terms to superintend its construction.

Arrangements have been made by which parties are now engaged in making, in the best style of the photographic art, views of each county in the State, including scenery along the rivers and railroads, the homes, school-houses, colleges, churches, public buildings, buildings of interest and manufacturing industries, averaging about seventy views in each county, together with the State buildings. It is designed to "decorate" the State building with about 7,000 of these views.

Each of the three political parties, holding State conventions, adopted a resolution favoring "a hearty co-operation by the people and a liberal appropriation by the next General Assembly, in order that the State may creditably exhibit her resources at the great gathering of the nations of the world."

Our Executive Committee is now engaged in preparing a detailed statement of the amount of the appropriation that will be needed to enable the Commission to make such an exhibit as will worthily represent Iowa among the States of the Union, and help to augment our national exhibit in its comparison with other nations.

Such detailed estimate, when adopted, will form part of our report to be presented to the next General Assembly.

JAMES O. CROSBY,
Representing Iowa Columbian Commission.

KENTUCKY.

MR. PRESIDENT, MADAME PRESIDENT: The Legislature of Kentucky, meeting only on alternate years, has not convened since the Exposition became an assured fact, consequently the State having had no opportunity to make an appropriation or appoint a commission, they can, therefore, send no formal report of accomplished work.

There is, however, no lack of strong, active interest in the Exposition, and there are encouraging indications that the present Legislature will be generous in its provision for an exhibit of the State's great resources at the Exposition. An enthusiastic meeting, touching our representation at the World's Fair, was recently held by the Commercial Club, of Louisville, which is the most important association of the character in Kentucky.

The National Commissioners and the Lady Managers of the State have done everything in their power to promote the enterprise, and are at present directing a united effort toward securing favorable legislation.

NANCY HUSTON BANKS.

KANSAS.

THOMAS W. PALMER, *President National Commission World's Columbian Exposition, Chicago, Ill.*

SIR: In compliance with the request for a statement of the progress made in the different States, as representative of the Board of Managers Kansas Exhibit, I beg leave to submit the following report:

A meeting called by the State Board of Agriculture convened and was held in the city of Topeka on the 23d and 24th days of April, 1891, for the purpose of devising plans to have Kansas properly represented at the World's Columbian Exposition at Chicago in 1893. A committee consisting of twenty-one members was elected and organized as a Bureau of Promotion, and vested with general authority to perform every service necessary to accomplish this purpose. They decided that a creditable exhibit of the products and resources of the State would require the expenditure of the sum of one hundred thousand dollars, and counties and railroad companies were asked to contribute such portion of this sum as the assessed value of their property bears to the assessed value of the property of the State. The response to this call was liberal, and, on the 16th day of September a convention, composed of delegates representing subscrip-

tions to the fund, assembled in the City of Topeka and elected a
permanent Board of Managers, composed of nine men and two
women. The Board of Managers organized at once and continued the work begun by the Board of Promotion. Their plan
is to form county Columbian Associations in every county in the
State, and have them continue in existence until the close of the
Exposition. These county organizations will collect necessary
funds, and collect products and materials, and co-operate in every
possible way with the Board of Managers in making a complete
exhibit of the products, resources, and progress of the State.
The members of the Board are now engaged in organizing
county associations, and are meeting with success. Railroad
companies and county associations representing one-half of the
required one hundred thousand dollars, have responded with the
first installment of their allotment of funds, and the work will
continue until the companies and counties are all interested in
the exhibit. Our county associations will encourage effort and
stir up a general interest in the enterprise. Kansas will come to
Chicago fully prepared to meet competition.

Respectfully submitted,

A. S. JOHNSON,
Representative.

MAINE.

To Hon. Geo. R. Davis, *Director General World's Columbian
Exposition:*

Sir: I have the honor, as representing the Maine Board of
World's Fair Managers, to state that the Act of the Maine Legislature, creating the Board, appropriated $40,000 for its use,
$10,000 of which must be used for erecting a State building. Sev-
eral plans for this building are now under consideration and will
be acted upon early in January. A copy of the Act of the Maine
Legislature is attached to this report. Nothing further has been
done under the State Act, except to elect officers of the Board, a
list of which is hereto attached. Immediately after January,
active measures will be taken to solicit exhibits.

The State Board is made up of eight members, four men and

four women, appointed by the Governor, with the members (and their alternates) of the National Board resident within the State as *ex-officio* members. The Executive Commissioner is a member of the State Board and is elected by the Board.

CHARLES P. MATTOCKS,
Representative Maine Board of World's Fair Managers.

MASSACHUSETTS.

The Massachusetts Board of Managers of the World's Columbian Exposition consists of five members, three men and two women. Its only organization is as follows: A Chairman and a Secretary who together form the Executive Committee of the Board. The Secretary is also the Executive Commissioner of the State, being appointed by the Board.

Our State appropriation is $75,000, of which $10,000 is specifically set apart for education.

Our Board conceives it to be its duty to solicit and obtain such exhibits from the State as shall best and most creditably show its natural resources and its material development in the several departments for which provisions have been made by the Chicago management.

The Board is further of the opinion that not only should such powers be given to the State Boards, but that they should be held to a strict accountability for the exhibits of their several States.

The only exhibit which it is designed to hold in the State Building is one which shall have for its object a consecutive and chronological history of the State, by the use of portraits of eminent citizens from the early settlers to the present time, as well as by maps, charts, and relics of colonial and revolutionary interest. The Board is doing what it can to popularize the Exposition by the use of circulars, personal interviews, and by a close cooperation with the many Boards of Trade and other mercantile associations to be found within our State.

The Board has had plans for the State Building prepared and has accepted the same. It is expected that the work upon this building will be commenced at an early day, and that nothing

5

will prevent its completion by October 12, 1892, the day set apart for the dedicatory ceremonies. The sum of $35,000 has been appropriated for this purpose, and it is the intention of the Board to erect a substantial building which shall externally, as well as by its internal furnishings, reflect credit upon the history and dignity of the commonwealth and serve in some degree, at least, to harmonize with the artistic conception of the architects and landscape gardens.

John W. Corcoran, *Chairman.*

E. C. Hovey, *Exposition Commissioner.*

MICHIGAN.

Report of I. M. Weston, President of the Board of World's Fair Managers of the State of Michigan.

December 10, 1891.

Mr. President: The Legislature of Michigan appropriated $100,000 for World's Fair purposes, and provided for a Board of Managers, to consist of four men, two women, and the Governor (ex-officio), with a salaried Secretary.

The first meeting, held August 5th, elected officers and appointed a Committee on By-Laws and Rules.

The next meeting was at Chicago the following week, when a site for a State building was accepted, a committee appointed to report building plans, and an appropriation of $20,000 made for construction.

At the September meeting, by-laws and rules were adopted, an Executive Committee of three was appointed, and quarterly meetings of the full Board provided for. The plan adopted for organizing the State, called for an auxiliary committee in every county, and special committees from the State at large for the leading classes of exhibitors. The county committees consist of three members, with one additional for each 10,000 inhabitants above the first 10,000. The work of the Board was divided into seven divisions, one of which was assigned to each member.

At the October meeting most of the committees were appointed, and each member of the Board was requested to make a careful estimate of the amount of financial aid required for the various class of exhibits, and report the same for consideration at the January meeting.

The lady members of the Board presented a draft of an address to the women of the State on their work, which was approved and ordered printed and distributed.

The lady members were also requested to prepare a plan of organization for the work of making a creditable Michigan exhibit in the Woman's Building.

Our plan called for the appointing of about 400 busy men and women on committees, yet the interest in the Fair is so great that nearly every nominee has accepted and is working with a will for success.

We commenced by soliciting exhibits, but during the past few weeks our principal work has been to hold back and restrict applications, as we find Michigan would gladly fill four times the space we can obtain.

In my own city there are forty-two large furniture factories, and nearly every one of them would send a train-load of goods, if you could take care of them.

Our farmers are thoroughly aroused and will make a great display. In the way of a fruit exhibit, we expect to repeat what we did at Philadelphia in 1876, viz.: beat the world.

Our mineral contributions will be in keeping with a State which leads all others in iron ore, salt, and gypsum, and is second, if not first, in copper.

As is well known, Michigan is the greatest lumbering State in the Union and will make a grand exhibition of forestry products.

Our fishery exhibit will also be interesting and extensive, and our specimens of manufactured goods will surpass most of the States in variety and extent.

Our educational institutions, headed by our grand State University, the largest in the United States, are already actively at work, and will make a fine showing.

I think I am safe in saying that among the States Michigan will rank next to Illinois in the quantity and quality of her exhibit at Chicago in 1893.   I. M. WESTON,
President.

MINNESOTA.

The Legislature of Minnesota, in the winter of 1890 and
1891, agreeable to an Act of Congress, passed a law for the
appointment of a Board of World's Fair Managers for Minnesota, said Commission to consist of six members, two from each
of the political parties—Democrat, Alliance, and Republican.
The members of the National Commission, together with the
Governor, to be members *ex-officio* of the State Board.   The law
creating such Commission provides that no member thereof shall
receive compensation for services or expenses, making their labor
one of pure patriotism.   An officer termed Superintendent of
Exhibit was provided for in the Act, and such officer was chosen
and is now engaged in the work under his charge.   The appropriation made by the Legislature for making an exhibit of the
resources and products of Minnesota, was limited to $50,000,
which, in the estimation of the State Board, after a review and
careful consideration of the situation, was deemed entirely
inadequate for the purposes; and to the end that a larger fund
might be secured, steps were taken, and an appeal made to the
people of the State, asking for $100,000 additional.   The method
inaugurated for securing this sum is by apportioning among the
various counties of the State an amount equal to 17-100 of a
mill on the dollar of assessed valuation, as returned by the
various assessors in 1890, leaving to each county to provide such
ways and means for raising its apportionment as might seem
most speedy and judicious.   This work was begun about five
weeks since, and we have now half of the counties of the State
that have either raised the amount apportioned or have committees appointed, who are at work, and give every assurance that
the amount will be raised.   With this money at hand, making a
total of $150,000, Minnesota will be enabled to present her
interests at the great Exposition of 1893 in a manner entirely
creditable to her.   Owing to the uncertainty as to what amount
of money would be at the disposal of the Board up to this date,
that body has deemed it expedient not to give publicity to a
plan for an exhibit until such period as the monetary considera-

tion might be settled; hence, in this particular, I have nothing to offer that could be of any value to this meeting.

There is no provision in our legislative enactment providing for the selection of a Board of Lady Managers, and no authority given for the setting aside of a sum for aiding the Woman's Department. Minnesota is, however, extremely fortunate in having very excellent and enthusiastic lady representatives on the National Board, and the State Board of Managers will, no doubt, afford these good ladies all the assistance in their power to aid them in the work of their department. If $100,000 shall be raised as above referred to, at least $5,000 thereof will be devoted to the uses and purposes of the Woman's Department, and will be expended under the direction of the Lady Commissioners on the National Board. Should this sum be insufficient for the purpose, woman's acuteness for devising ways and means to relieve such embarrassment may be relied upon to furnish a remedy. Respectfully submitted,

L. P. HUNT,
Superintendent State Exhibit.

MISSOURI.

MR. PRESIDENT : The Missouri Board of World's Fair Commissioners is the creation of an Act of the Missouri Legislature, composed of seven appointees of the Governor of the State. The appropriation is $150,000. The Board has one salaried agent—an Executive Commissioner. It has an Auxiliary Board of ladies, which has control of the work in which women will participate at the Exposition.

The Missouri Board was organized August 7th, and since that time has met monthly in different parts of the State to arouse popular interest in the Exposition. This plan has created the greatest possible enthusiasm. The office of the President is at Sedalia. The headquarters of the Board, at Kansas City, is joined by direct telephone connection with that of the President, 125 miles away. The office of the Vice-President is at St. Louis, as is that of the Executive Commission. The head-

quarters of the Ladies' Auxiliary is at St. Joe, Mo. The work
has progressed very rapidly.

Missouri has regularly organized associations of agriculture,
horticulture, live stock, and others; these, with the State Bureaus
representing other of her interests, are all actively engaged in
the work ; but now this work has come to a complete standstill
owing to the delay in fixing the site for Missouri Building to
which, in justice and fairness, she is entitled. Whatever may be
done in the direction of continuing of the work, hereafter, will
depend entirely on the prompt action of the properly constituted
authorities here. Respectfully,

MATHEW FRANK.

MONTANA.

To the President of the World's Columbian Commission:

In compliance with the resolution adopted requesting the
representatives of the different State Boards to report the progress made in furtherance of the World's Exposition, as the representative of the State of Montana I have to report that the
State Board of Managers have organized in conformity with the
law of the State, and have appointed committees representing
the leading industries of the State, with directions to gather
statistical and other information showing the development,
progress, and resources of the State. It is too early to state
definitely what has yet been accomplished, but these committees
will no doubt, at the proper time, present full reports, showing
the development, progress, and resources of the State, and
especially present accurate and full details of its great mineral
wealth.

The collection of exhibits is in the hands of an Executive
Commissioner, who, with a corps of assistants has already
begun the work of collecting exhibits. It is confidently believed
that in many of the cereals Montana will rank with any of the
other States; while in the extent and variety of her mineral
exhibits she will surpass any of them.

The amount appropriated by the State for the Columbian
Exposition is $50,000. This sum is inadequate to make as

complete an exhibit as would be desirable, and pay the necessary expenses incident thereto. It will be for the next Legislature of the State, which will meet in January, 1893, to decide whether an additional appropriation shall be made.

A matter in which the State Board of Montana, and many others, feel much interest, is the allotment of a site for a State building. Some confusion or misconception has arisen in regard to this, which it is unnecessary here to recount. But it is earnestly desired that the question be settled as quickly as possible, and that Montana may be allotted the site originally promised.

A plan of a State building has been prepared and is ready to be submitted for approval as soon as it is definitely determined where the building shall be placed.

Respectfully submitted,

S. De Wolfe,
President Montana State Board of Managers.

Chicago, Dec. 9, 1891.

NEW HAMPSHIRE.

Geo. R. Davis, *Director General World's Columbian Exposition, Chicago.*

Dear Sir: As Executive Commissioner of the World's Fair Commissioners of our State, I have the honor of making the following report:

The Legislature, at its session last winter, made an appropriation of $25,000, and stipulated that $10,000 should be expended in the erection of a State building. The plans of this building have not yet been accepted, but the building will be erected early the coming summer.

Under this law the Governor appointed four Commissioners, all men. No provision was made recognizing any of the members of the National Commission or the Lady Members or their Alternates. We have, however, invited them to our meetings, and expect they will work in harmony with the State Board.

With the exception of the appointment of a few important committees, the work of the Board has so far been of an organizing character. We confidently expect to make a creditable display of our natural and manufactured products, and our State will do all in its power to assist in carrying forward the great Exposition, in which we all have a mutual interest.

Yours truly,   E. M. SHAW,
Ex-Commissioner.

NEBRASKA.

CHICAGO, December 10, 1891.

DIRECTOR GENERAL GEORGE R. DAVIS, *World's Columbian Exposition, Chicago, Ill.*

MY DEAR SIR: Nebraska begs leave to make the following report: The Legislature of Nebraska made an appropriation during their session, in 1891, of $50,000, to be used in making a State exhibit at the World's Columbian Exposition, to be held in Chicago during the year 1893. The 1st of August, 1891, the Governor of Nebraska appointed six Commissioners and one Commissioner General to take charge and look after said exhibit. Since August 1st, the Nebraska Commission have visited most of the counties in the State and organized a County World's Fair Commission, to work in connection with the State Commission, and while we find an earnest desire, especially among our farmers, to assist in making up a fine exhibit, there is also a very earnest demand that the State be allowed to place not only cereals, and other products of the soil, in the State building, but also any manufactured articles, from those products, that may be desired; as well as fine arts, and woman's handiwork. It is the opinion of the Nebraska State Commission, and also their constituents, that unless this privilege is granted they could not make such a display and showing up of the State as would be beneficial and satisfactory to all concerned. We have no plans for our State building to submit for your approval as yet; the delay has been contingent on your final decision in the matters above referred to. Respectfully yours,

R. R. GREER,
Commissioner General.

A. L. STRANG,
President.

NEW JERSEY.

REPORT OF NEW JERSEY COMMISSION.

In compliance with the resolution adopted yesterday, the committee representing the New Jersey Commission of the World's Columbian Exposition make the following report, to wit:

During the session of 1891, of the Legislature of New Jersey, a bill was passed authorizing the appointment of eight Commissioners, to be known as the New Jersey Commission of the World's Columbian Exposition, who were to assist the various Boards of the State in making their respective exhibits and to encourage the manufacturers throughout the State to make such displays of their productions as would reflect credit upon them and uphold the reputation of New Jersey in all of her manufacturing interests.

For wise reasons, but twenty thousand ($20,000) dollars was asked for in this bill; which amount was appropriated.

The Commissioners were duly appointed, and since their organization have been steadily at work.

It has been decided to erect a building on the plot of ground allotted to New Jersey, at a cost not to exceed $20,000, the building to be constructed of materials produced in the State, and probably so planned that its parts may be gotten out and fitted in New Jersey, brought to Jackson Park, and erected by workmen from our State. In order to do this, and all the work devolving upon the Commission, an enlarged appropriation is inevitable, for which we look to the Legislature convening "early in January, 1892;" and we expect a sum adequate for all uses.

Feeling that we could best induce our people to exhibit, our Commission, through its Secretary, has obtained blank forms of application for space from the Director General and sent them to our manufacturers.

We regret to state that the returns have been few thus far. We propose to issue a circular letter, in the very near future, to the intending exhibitors of New Jersey, containing not only an urgent appeal, but some valuable information, gathered at this conference.

The law authorizing the New Jersey Commission does not contemplate a Board of Lady Managers. Such an addition may be made at the coming session of the Legislature.

(Signed)   F. J. MEEKER,
WALTER F. LENOX,
Committee.

NEW MEXICO.

The Board of Managers of the World's Columbian Exposition of New Mexico met and organized in pursuance of the Territorial law under which it was created.

Owing to an omission in the law, the appropriation of $25,000 made by the Territory will not become available until 1892.

This omission has greatly retarded the action of the Territorial Board. The Act authorized each county to make an additional appropriation.

The Board has, however, organized, formulated the course to be pursued, appointed its committees, and entered upon the work with a determination to present as fully as possible the wonderful natural resources of the Territory.

An especial effort is being made to exhibit its varied and vast mineral wealth, its precions stones and rare gems; the variety and extent of its forestry, the variety and quality of agricultural and horticultural products, viniculture, and manufactured wine.

To the collection and exhibition of an archæological and ethnological display, as gathered from the abandoned ruins of the Cliff Dwellers, the Pueblo and Aztec Indians.

And to make a practical exhibit of the mode of farming in the arid regions by means of irrigation.

The work has been divided among the different members of the Board; agents have been appointed and placed in the field under the control of the Board to collect and prepare the various exhibits; Boards and committees have been organized in many of the counties, and a spirit of local emulation aroused by the offering of premiums to be paid by the Territory.

The Territorial Board has decided to join the other Territories in the erection of a joint building for the use of all the Territories; an appropriation has been made for this purpose, and the plans and specifications of the proposed building prepared and submitted to the Director General and Board of Construction for approval.

W. T. Thornton,
President Board of Managers for New Mexico.

NORTH DAKOTA.

Chicago, Ill., December 10, 1891.

To the Chairman of the Conference of the Boards of Control and State Representatives:

As the representative of the State of North Dakota, I have the honor to report that the Legislature of our State, at its session last winter, made an appropriation of $25,000 for the purposes of making our exhibit at the World's Fair, erecting State buildings, etc.

In justice to our Legislature I would state that the framers of our State Constitution, in fixing upon a per cent. upon the valuation of the State as a basis for establishing the maximum indebtedness to be allowed, settled upon a rate which, while it would be tolerable, perhaps, for older and established States, was ridiculous in a State about to commence housekeeping on its own account. The constitution will be amended in this respect as soon as the established course of procedure will permit. Meantime, with rich resources in the State, all enterprises dependent upon appropriation were hampered, in view of which fact the friends of the Exposition in North Dakota asked only for the $25,000 which was allowed.

We hope to have a further appropriation at the next session of our Legislature, but this has not and will not interfere with the arrangements which we have made to raise funds by contribution.

Acting upon the suggestion of National Commissioner Rucker,

we have started a popular $1 subscription for the purpose of raising funds for our State building. We propose later on to ask for general subscriptions to add to the general fund of which we have control.

Our Board unanimously adopted plans for a State building, furnished us by J. L. Silsbee, Esq., and the matter is now in his hands, the building to be erected at such times as may be desired by the Construction Department.

Little has as yet been done in the way of collecting or preparing exhibits, except in the way of flora.

Our North Dakota Millers' Association and Live Stock & Dairy Association have already shown a lively interest in the Exposition, and will do all in their power to make the exhibits in their several branches a success.

With respect to the Woman's Department I have to report that our State Board authorized the National Lady Managers of our State to organize the ladies of North Dakota into World's Columbian Exposition Circles, and this work is now progressing satisfactorily.

In the Department of Education and Forestry, I am gratified to report that our State has made much progress. The State Superintendent of Public Instruction and the State Superintendent of Forestry have taken charge of their respective departments with intelligence and energy, and have already accomplished all necessary preliminary work.

Our State Board consists of five members, appointed by the Governor. The National members—ladies and gentlemen—are ex-officio members.   Respectfully submitted,

H. C. SOUTHARD,
President of State Board, N. Dak.

OHIO.

Madam President, Mr. President, Ladies and Gentlemen of the Conference:

I had not expected to make any report. I came to learn, and hoped that some gentleman of our Board would have been present to tell you what our State has been doing for the Columbian Commission; but, none having come, I present the following slight sketch of our Appropriation Bill and the little that we have, so far, been able to accomplish in our State.

An Act to provide for the collection, arrangement, and display of the products of the State of Ohio, at the World's Columbian Exposition of 1893, was passed by the General Assembly of the State of Ohio, March 21, 1891. This Act has for its basis a bill, formulated, I have understood, by the National Commission, and makes an appropriation of $100,000 for the State work in the Commission.

Early in April, the Governor appointed the members of the State Board, agreeably to the provisions of the bill. This Board consists of twenty-three members, including the National Commissioners and their alternates, and the Lady Managers and their alternates.

The Board held its first meeting at Columbus, on the 8th day of April, 1891. We elected a President, W. W. Peabody, Esq., and a Secretary at this first meeting. No Executive Commissioner has, as yet, been elected. So far, the duties which would have devolved upon such an officer have been ably discharged by our very efficient President and Secretary. It has, however, been decided to elect one at the February meeting of the State Board.

The scope of the work of the Board of Ohio's World's Fair Managers is outlined as follows:

(1) To obtain necessary information regarding the Exposition from the officers thereof and disseminate the same through the State.

(2) To secure a complete and creditable display of the interests of the State at the Exposition.

(3) To solicit, collect, transport, prepare, arrange, and exhibit objects sent to the Exposition under authority of the State for the purpose of exhibiting the resources, history, progress, welfare, products, and general development of the State.

(4) To exercise full authority in relation to the participation of the State and its citizens in the Exposition.

(5) To transport, arrange, and exhibit, at the expense of the owners, objects placed in charge of the Board by individual citizens.

(6) To provide a State Headquarters at the Exposition.

Neither the President, Vice-President, nor Commissioners receive any compensation, except for necessary traveling expenses and per diem, when absent from home on business of the State Board.

The President of the Board has arranged twenty-three committees, consisting each of three members. Each committee has a chairman appointed by the President.

It has been decided by the State Board that none of the money, already appropriated by the General Assembly of Ohio, can be used except for State exhibits proper. We have had several discussions in regard to the amount which each of these State Societies should receive, in order to make their exhibits with credit to the State—such as the agricultural and horticultural, the historical and archæological, the educational exhibits, etc., etc.

At the last meeting a "Budget Committee" was appointed, whose duty it will be to apportion the money, so that no one State Society shall receive more than its share of the public money to the detriment of the others, except as to the Ohio Building; for this a definite sum has been already appropriated. The Building Committee have, with the approval of the Board, employed an architect from the State Board of Architects to construct this building. It is designed to use, in its construction, only the products of Ohio. I am not able to say how far the work on the building has progressed. We hope to make it pleasant headquarters for people from Ohio, and we shall, also, hope to extend its hospitalities to our sister States and people of other nationalities.

There has not been mapped out, as yet, any line of women's

special work for Ohio. A committee has been appointed to draw up a plan for this work. There will, probably, be a small sum appropriated for this work. There will not be, I presume, a great deal done by Ohio women in this direction. They are employed in so many avocations jointly with men, and belong to so many art associations, schools of art, colleges of music, etc., etc., each and all of which will, no doubt, make their own exhibits.

It may seem as if the people of Ohio were a little slow in grasping the great possibilities of the Columbian Exposition, but Ohio will come on in time and leave her work in the history of the World's Fair.

I will not detain you with a résumé of the resources of our State and the embarrassment of riches from which she can furnish exhibits worthy of the occasion, but will leave her to speak for herself in 1893.

MARY A. HART,
Member of the State Board of Ohio.
World's Columbian Exposition.

PENNSYLVANIA.

HON. THOS. W. PALMER, *President:*

Pennsylvania was among the first States to respond to your call with an appropriation of $300,000 and the appointment of a Board of Managers, with Governor Pattison as presiding officer. Committees were selected and organized, in accordance with your first classification, and subsequently rearranged after your revision. Our committees are now all organized and at work under the general direction of our efficient executive officer, Benjamin Whitman. Seventy-five thousand dollars have been appropriated for our State Building. The architect's plans are now in the hands of the Executive Committee. Our Board of Managers have been meeting the second Thursday in each month. The meetings have been largely attended and enthusiastic; but, as our business is now fully organized, it is proposed that we meet bi-monthly, and our committees semi-monthly. We are doing all in our power to interest citizens generally in the cause, offering premiums for the best display of cereals, tobacco, and such products as would not be exhibited by private enterprise for commercial purposes; and, in short, are stirring up and keeping alive a sentiment of State pride among the people, with a view of securing the most complete and creditable display of Pennsylvania products that it is possible to gather together. The work in the Women's Department is further advanced and better organized than any other. Miss McCandless is here to speak of that. Respectfully,

A. B. FARQUHAR.

REPORT—MISS McCANDLESS, PENNSYLVANIA.

The ladies of the National Board are members of the State Board, and Mrs. Mabel C. Jones has also been elected a member. Auxiliary Societies are being formed in the twenty-six congressional districts, from five to fifteen women composing a District Committee. After receiving their commissions, the said committees will meet in their respective districts, receive instructions from the Executive Commissioner, Mr. Whitman, and each Committee will elect a District Delegate, who will confer with the Committee on Women's Work.

1st. The said committee to see the importance of a general circular, informing the women of the several States what they will be allowed to exhibit, and what is expected of them.

2d. Weekly reports of the exhibitors who have applied from each State.

3d. A systematic plan which will result in bringing together the best results of women's work, without duplicating articles that are of common use, and of no special interest except to those who made them or in the localities where they are produced.

4th. The necessity for prompt and satisfactory communication with the Executive Commissioners of the various States, so that they may know at all times what is being done in the Women's Department, and be guided accordingly.

RHODE ISLAND.

To the Board of Reference and Control of the National Commission and the World's Columbian Exposition.

I beg leave to report: On the 4th of August, 1891, the Legislature of Rhode Island passed an Act to provide for the collection, arrangement, and display of the products of the State of Rhode Island at the World's Columbian Exposition of 1893, and to make an appropriation therefor. The first section of this Act provided:

"SECTION 1. That for the purpose of exhibiting the resources, products, and general development of the State of Rhode Island at the World's Columbian Exposition of 1893, a Commission is hereby constituted, to be designated, "The Board of World's Fair Managers of Rhode Island," which shall consist of the World's Columbian Commissioners from this State and their alternates, and the Board of Lady Managers of the World's Columbian Commission from this State, and their alternates, and the World's Columbian Commissioner at large and alternate from the State, if any there be, and eight citizens, to be organized and continue its duties as hereinafter provided.

"SEC. 2. The eight citizen members of said Board shall be appointed by the Governor, in equal number, from the two leading parties, within thirty days after the passage of this Act, and shall meet at such time as the Governor may appoint, and organize by the election of a President, a Vice-President, a Secretary, and a Treasurer. Five members of said Board shall constitute a quorum for the transaction of business. The Board shall have power to make rules and regulations for its government, provided such rules and regulations will not conflict with the regulations adopted under the Act of Congress for the government of said World's Columbian Exposition. Any member of the Board may be removed at any time by the Governor, for cause. Any vacancy which may occur in the membership of said Board shall be filled by the Governor.

"SEC. 5. The said Board shall have charge of the interests of the State and its citizens in the preparation and exhibition, at the

6

World's Columbian Exposition of 1893, of the natural and industrial products of the State, and of objects illustrating its history, progress, moral and material welfare, and future development, and in all other matters relating to said World's Columbian Exposition; it shall communicate with the officers of, and obtain and disseminate through the State, all necessary information regarding said Exposition, and in general have and exercise full authority in relation to the participation of the State of Rhode Island and its citizens in the World's Columbian Exposition of 1893.

"SEC. 7. To carry out the provisions of this Act, the sum of $25,000, or as much thereof as may be necessary, is hereby appropriated out of any money in the treasury not otherwise appropriated."

The location allotted by the Director General for the Rhode Island State Building has been accepted by the Commission, and a plan for such building has been submitted to the Chief of the Bureau of Construction for his approval. Under the new conditions, which I believe are to result from this Conference, I have no doubt that the contributions from the State I have the honor to represent will be more numerous and important.

Many of our large manufacturers of cotton and woolen goods, of steam engines and machinery, have already expressed their intention to make exhibits on a scale which I am sure will add to the attraction of the Exposition, and reflect credit on my State.

JOHN C. WYMAN,
Executive Commissioner.

SOUTH DAKOTA.

MR. PRESIDENT:—The South Dakota World's Fair Commission begs leave to submit, as the major part of its report, the annexed pamphlet, which contains nearly all the information asked for by the resolution of yesterday, offered by the member of the Board of Control from California.

Since the pamphlet was printed, there has been appointed a Lady Commission of eight members, which will meet at Huron the 17th inst. for the election of the usual executive officers, and one Lady Commissioner for the State at large. The names of the officers and members of the Lady Commission will be printed in the second edition of the pamphlet, should such issue be deemed advisable. The first edition is 10,000 copies, a sufficient number of which are placed on the table here to supply the State Commissions present, with whom we hereby solicit an exchange of documents.

As the pamphlet outlines our plan of a State collective exhibit, it may not be amiss to report in this connection that the plan has been adopted by the Commission as its chart and compass, and stands as the pledge of the Commission to the people of the State, of whom it is asking voluntary contributions to the amount of $80,000. We are unable to see how such an exhibit can be made in the name of, and fully to the credit of, our State under the present plan of the Exposition, which we have studied carefully. We offer no captious opposition; we merely state a fact.

We further report that what our people seem to desire is that we produce a collective State exhibit that shall be installed by the Commission in its own way, subject only to obviously necessary general rules; an exhibit that shall remain under the control of the State Commission, subject to the rules mentioned, and be presented to the world by said Commission, entirely free from the control or interference of the competitive departments.

While saying this, we desire to state also that we are equally ambitious that the competitive departments shall be filled, and our people and our Commission will do their share to fill them.

Respectfully submitted,

OLIVER GIBBS, JR.,
Delegate and General Manager.

Approved by:

CHAS. E. BAKER, *Commissioner.*

ROBT. B. FISK, *Secretary of Commission.*

Present at this conference.

TENNESSEE.

The delegates of the World's Fair Managers of Tennessee respectfully report that the State of Tennessee has made no appropriation for a building or exhibit at the Exposition, but has authorized appropriations to be made by the counties, and has appointed a "Board of World's Fair Managers," without provision for any compensation, or even a fund for expenses. If funds are raised, actual expenses of members may be paid and officers may have compensation.

This Board consists of the Governor of the State, the members of the National Board for the State, and fifteen members, of whom six are women, appointed by the Governor. These have authority to appoint an executive manager, but are not required to do so.

This Board met in Nashville on Tuesday, the 3d day of November, last, and organized by the election of O. P. Temple, of Knox County, President; C. W. Tyler, of Montgomery, Vice-President; Daniel Bond, of Haywoods, Secretary; and Lewis T. Baxter, of Davidson, Treasurer.

An Executive Committee was appointed, consisting of the officers of the Board, and J. B. Heiskell, Chairman, and Mrs. Carrington Mason, of Shelby County; E. C. Mowell and Mrs. M. C. Goodlet, of Davidson; John T. Wilder, of Washington, and Mrs. Sam. McKinney, of Knox.

Efforts are being made in the principal cities of the State to induce liberal appropriations by the County Courts, and influential exchanges and public bodies have recommended prompt and liberal action, and we think we have reasonable ground to hope that we may realize $50,000, or perhaps $100,000, to erect a State building and make a State exhibit.

Our County Courts can act upon appropriations only at their quarterly terms, the first of which occurs on the first Monday of January next, that being the first term since the organization of the State Board, so that it has not been possible to procure any action up to this time. In several of the wealthiest and most populous counties we expect to obtain action at the January term, but in many of the counties it can not be expected that action can be procured until April. If, however, the counties of Davidson, Hamilton, Knox, Montgomery, and Shelby can be induced, in January, to make liberal appropriations, it will give assurance of a respectable exhibit.

Respectfully submitted,

O. P. TEMPLE,
J. B. HEISKELL.

TEXAS.

HON. T. W. PALMER, *President World's Fair Conference.*

SIR: As a member of the Board of Directors of the Texas World's Fair Exhibit Association; authorized and requested to represent said Board at this conference and in compliance with the resolution adopted yesterday, I have the honor to submit the following:

When the Legislature of Texas adjourned last winter without making an appropriation to have the State creditably represented at the World's Columbian Exposition, the people of Texas held a convention in the city of Fort Worth and organized the Texas World's Fair Exhibit Association, with a capital stock of $300,000 divided into shares of $1 each. A board of seven directors, one from each of the seven larger cities of the State, was chosen by the convention. These directors immediately secured a charter for the association and went to work to raise the $300,000 by dividing it up among the 220 counties in the State on a basis of 15 cents per capita. More than half these counties have already raised their quota.

Texas, through its popular organization, will spend $100,000 on its State building, which will be built of Texas woods, granite, marble, limestone, iron, brick, and other native materials. The plans for this building have just been adopted. One hundred thousand dollars will be expended in stocking this building with county collective exhibits of its natural products and resources and a very extensive historical exhibit of Texas as a province of Mexico, as an independent republic, and as one of the States of the Union. These exhibits will be made in harmony with the rules adopted by the Board of Control with reference to State exhibits. The Board of Directors of the Texas Association have more fully recognized the participation of women in World's Fair work than has thus far been done by any other State, having arranged for a convention of the women of Texas, which was held in Dallas on October 29th, and which was honored and encouraged by the presence of the President of the National Board of Lady Managers, who addressed the women on World's Fair work. At this meeting the Texas Board of Lady Managers was organized by the election of a President and Secretary, and the President appointed an Executive Committee of thirty-one women, representing each of the State senatorial districts.

Local committees of men and women are now thoroughly organized and heartily and enthusiastically at work in each of the 220 counties in the State, and report weekly to the officers of the association at their headquarters at Waco. From the great success that these county committees are meeting with, both in raising money and promoting the interests of the Exposition, it is believed that this method of securing funds to have a State creditably represented at the World's Fair will achieve grander, more effective results than appropriations made by a State Legislature, and will be the means of bringing forth the largest number of suitable and acceptable exhibits, both from the State itself as well as its individual citizens, to be shown in the departmental buildings of the Exposition, in the Woman's Building, and in the State Building.

Texas, on this occasion, desires to return its sincere thanks to Director General Davis and to Mrs. President Palmer for having visited the State—the former in May last and the latter in October—and by their presence and influence rendering the popular World's Fair movement in Texas an assured success.

JNO. T. DICKINSON.

VERMONT.

Pursuant to the resolution adopted December 9, 1891, the following report is presented from the World's Columbian Commission of Vermont:

At a special session of the Legislature of Vermont, held in August, 1891, the sum of $15,000 was appropriated for Exposition uses, and an Act was passed under which a Commission of nine members has been appointed, of which the Governor of the State is Chairman, the other members being the Commissioners, the alternate Commissioners, Lady Managers, and alternate Lady Managers who had been previously designated. The organization of the World's Columbian Commission of Vermont has been completed by the appointment of H. H McIntyre as General Agent. Arrangements are in progress for the erection of a building and for the preparation of a State exhibit.   All of which is respectfully submitted,

ALDACE F. WALKER,
Commissioner.

WASHINGTON.

To the Officers and Members of the National Commission and of the World's Columbian Exposition and of the Board of Lady Managers, to the Delegates from the different State associations here assembled.

LADIES AND GENTLEMEN: Knowing that by the time the report from the State of Washington is reached we will all be fully tired out and exhausted, I beg to state that while I feel that our new Western State is fully in line with the front ranks of the procession, I would confine myself in this report to a very general outline of what has been accomplished by our State.

Those taking an active interest in this work, instigated and agitated in August, 1890, a movement which succeeded in arousing a general feeling in almost every county, sending a special delegate to organize commercial organizations where none existed, which resulted in a delegated convention of one hundred, meeting for permanent organization at the Capitol of our State during the session of the Legislature in January, 1891.

The result of the work of this organization can be fully appreciated when it is stated that we obtained an appropriation of one hundred thousand ($100,000) dollars as a starter for the Washington Exhibit. We then formed a permanent organization under the name of the Washington World's Fair Commission, and by an Act passed by our Legislature. I submit herewith a copy of same and all rules and regulations under which we are working.

I am pleased to state that our general work is progressing more than satisfactorily. We have just had the plans for our building, which will be built entirely of Washington resources, formally approved by the supervising architects of Chicago.

We have every department of our State thoroughly organized, with a carefully chosen head, and while we are one of the newest, and financially one of the smallest, we expecf to show that we are made out of the kind of material that will continue to be awake to every proposition calculated to increase the strength and character of our nation.

Supposing that every question that I desire to ask will have been thought of before, I shall leave that portion from my report and ask the indulgence, in case any question presents itself, that I may be allowed the privilege of raising it hereafter.

Respectfully submitted,
PERCY W. ROCHESTER,
Of Washington.

WEST VIRGINIA.

Mr. President, Ladies and Gentlemen:

In conformity to the resolution passed at your meeting yesterday, of which I was informed late yesterday afternoon, not being present at the meeting, I beg to report, as the representative of the State Commission of West Virginia, that at the earliest opportunity at the meeting of our last Legislature that honorable body made an appropriation of $40,000, which is now available to aid its citizens in making a creditable display of the State's various resources, including its manufactured articles as well as its agricultural products, at the Columbian Exposition to be held in this city in 1893; and with this appropriation, a Commission composed of five gentlemen was to be appointed by the Governor to carry out the law creating said Commission. The said Commission was duly appointed, and has been in a state of organization since May last, since which time they have been actively engaged in working up the general State interest in this great Exposition, and I am glad to report that our people are taking a lively interest in the same.

In the appropriation made by our State, the Commission is limited in its expenditure to $20,000 for State building, and in this regard I am pleased to report that plans have been adopted which have been executed by our architect and approved by the Board of Control, and are now in the hands of builders, looking to an early completion of the same; and when completed, we expect and hope that it will reflect credit on our young and growing State, as well as to the general features of the Exposition.

Our exhibition will be of a character confined largely to our extensive manufactures, our almost inexhaustible resources as to timber, coal, and other minerals, which, heretofore, have been largely inaccessible, but are now being reached by the new railroads being projected and built throughout our State, the exhibition of which will be so opportune in connection with this great Exposition, the fact of which is very keenly appreciated by our whole people.

In conclusion, I desire to say that West Virginia will not be behind her sister States in her contribution to make this Exposition a grand success, and will always be found ready to co-operate with the controlling powers in accomplishing the great object for which this Exposition was inaugurated.

Respectfully submitted,

W. N. CHANCELLOR.

WISCONSIN.

MR. PRESIDENT: The amount appropriated by the Wisconsin Legislature for World's Fair work is $65,000. The Board consists of eleven members, seven of them having been appointed by the Governor and the remaining four being the National Commissioners and Lady Managers from the State.

The Board have elected Robert B. Kirkland, of Jefferson, Wis., as Executive Commissioner, who is now actively discharging the duties required of him.

Plans for a State Headquarters Building were accepted by the Board on October 20, 1891, and have, since that date, been duly and formally approved by the Bureau of Construction of the Exposition. It is estimated that the building will cost $30,000, and will be constructed entirely of Wisconsin material. Bids for the construction of the building will be asked for on February 15th, and actual erection of the same will begin early in the spring.

The Board have adopted a plan of appointing, in each of the sixty-eight counties of the State, a County Auxiliary Committee, to consist of two women and three men, whose duty shall be to co-operate with the State Board, attend to securing exhibits, and work up, in their respective localities, interest in the Exposition. These committees are to be announced and published on the 15th inst.

A very general interest in World's Fair work is being manifested throughout the State, and the people of Wisconsin keenly feel and appreciate that the proximity of the Fair to its borders will prove of material permanent advantage to the State.

C. W. GRAVES.

The questions presented by the representatives of the several States and referred to the Director General, were replied to as follows :

DIRECTOR GENERAL DAVIS:—It is evident, from the questions propounded, that this body does not thoroughly understand our organization.

We have, as you understand, a great work here to perform. The Board of Directors are taking charge of the buildings, through the Construction Department, and are pushing forward the work. They have charge, in their Committees, of all concessions, and matters of revenue come directly under their supervision. We also have an organization provided by compact between the National Board and the Board of Directors, to conduct the work of the Exposition. There are thirteen active executive Departments and two administrative Departments. Each one of these Departments has a Chief, and these Chiefs have been appointed with the greatest care. We have selected them from among the most noted men in their lines in this country.

We have at the head of the Department of Agriculture, Mr. W. I. Buchanan, of Iowa, a man well versed and expert in his line. The Department of Horticulture is under the charge of Mr. Samuels, of Kentucky. We had some difficulty in finding a Chief of that Department, but finally secured a very good one. He has associated with him in charge of the Bureau of Horticulture Mr. John Thorpe, of New York City, who is well known as a prominent floriculturist. Mr. Buchanan is acting Chief of the Department of Live Stock, but Mr. E. W. Cottrell, of Detroit, has been appointed Chief of that Department, and he will assume his duties in time to attend to all applications that are sent in. Captain J. W. Collins, in the Fish and Fisheries Department, was appointed by permission of the President of the United States from the National Fish Commission. He will look after not only the National but the State exhibits. The Department of Mines and Mining has Mr. F. J. V. Skiff, of Colorado, for Chief, who is well versed in the work of his Department. The Department of Machinery is under the charge of Gen. L. W. Robinson, detailed by the Secretary of the United States Navy for this duty. He was first officer under General Albert, who was superintendent of the Machinery Department of the Centennial, and is thoroughly qualified to go ahead with the work of his Department. Mr. Willard A. Smith, of Chicago, is in charge of the Department of Transportation Exhibits. The Manufactures Department is under Mr. James Allison, who was head of the great Exposition at Cincinnati. He is well versed in the work, and has great experience in expositions. Prof. John P. Barrett, of this city, has charge of the Department of Electricity. The Fine Arts Department is under the charge of Prof. H. W. Ives, of Washington University, St. Louis, who is abroad now in the interest of his Department. Dr. S. H. Peabody, late president of the University of Illinois, is in charge of the Department of Liberal Arts, which includes the Bureaus of Education, Music, and the Drama. Mr. Theodore Thomas has been appointed Musical Director and Mr. Thomas Tomlins Choral Director of the Bureau of Music. Prof. F. W. Putnam, of Harvard University, Chief of the Department of Ethnology, has given twenty-five years of his life to the special line of work under his charge, and is probably as excellent a Chief for that Department as we could find in this country. The Chiefs of the Departments of Publicity and Promotion and Foreign Affairs are respectively Major M. P. Handy, of Pennsylvania, and Hon. Walker Fearn, of Louisiana, late Minister to Greece, Roumania, and Servia.

I refer to the organization at this time for the purpose of showing that we have experts in charge of the work. They have under them a corps of employés located here, and assistants in other parts of the United States, and foreign countries, to attend to securing exhibits.

QUESTIONS AND ANSWERS.

CALIFORNIA.—1. What privileges will be granted to States and Territories to maintain within their respective buildings a café or restaurant where the products of their own State can be disposed of?

No provision has been made for such privileges.

2. In the matter of perishable goods, particularly in the Department of Horticulture, where they will have to be replaced frequently, will the exhibitors be allowed to dispose of their exhibits before they become a loss, and replace them with fresh exhibits from day to day?

Arrangements may be made with the Chief of any Department for the sale of perishable exhibits, under the regulations prescribed by the Ways and Means Committee.

3. In States or Territories where the Legislature have not provided for an Auxiliary Board of Lady Managers, is it desirable for the State Boards or Commission to organize such boards, or leave the work to be done by members of the National Board of Lady Managers from their respective States or Territories?

(Answer by Mrs. Potter Palmer, President of the Board of Lady Managers.)

It is very desirable for the State Boards to appoint auxiliary committees, as they can be remunerated from the funds of the State; and they are especially urged to appoint the Lady Managers and their alternates to full membership on these committees, and thus avoid many complications that would otherwise arise.

COLORADO.—1. Will permission be given to sell in State buildings, photographs of State scenery, books of native flora, etc., provided the consent of the State boards is secured?

No provision has been made for the sale of such articles in State buildings.

2. Will the names of exhibitors making displays through the State boards be allowed on their exhibits?

They will.

FLORIDA.—1. What will be the switching charge at Chicago from the depot of delivery to the World's Fair Grounds?

SWITCHING RATE ON EXHIBITS AT CHICAGO.—The switching rate on exhibits at Chicago, from the intersection of the various railroads with the Illinois Central tracks, will be eight (8) cents per 100 pounds.

This rate was agreed upon by the Committee on Transportation, subject to the approval of the Executive Committee, to whom the matter has been referred, and of whose action due notice will be given.

This rate will be made in both directions, and includes the switching rate both outside and within the Exposition grounds; also the placing of exhibits on or adjacent to the space allotted in the various buildings.

It is the intention that the terminal charge of eight (8) cents per 100 on the forward journey be prepaid, and collected with the freight charges at the point of shipment, the goods being delivered at the Exposition free of all charges.

SWITCHING RATE ON CONSTRUCTION MATERIAL AT CHICAGO. —The switching rate on construction material from the intersection of the Illinois Central road to the Exposition grounds, is six (6) dollars per car, in addition to. the regular freight rates, except on such cars as may be delivered to the Illinois Central road at Harvey and the Union Stock Yards, on which the rate will be seven (7) dollars per car. The above rates cover the expense of switching within the Exposition grounds to a point as near the State buildings as can be conveniently reached by the tracks now or hereafter constructed.

2. Will the switching rates on freight shipped by State boards be the same rate charged as on freight shipped by individual exhibitors?

A uniform switching rate will be made at Chicago for the handling of construction material and exhibits to both State and individual exhibitors.

ILLINOIS—1. Will the Illinois Board of World's Fair Commissioners be permitted to install and conduct a restaurant in one of the upper stories of their State building, for the exclusive use of and accommodation of the members of the Board and their employees?

No provision has been made for such privileges in State buildings.

2. What are the standards of admission for the several classes of animals, and especially the methods adopted in applying those standards, in deciding upon applications for entry? In other words, to what extent and by what authority will discrimination be exercised in deciding upon the acceptance or rejection of individual applications for entry of animals in the several classes included in the general classification for international competition?

The general standards of admission for live stock exhibits are presented in full in the printed regulations of that Department. The right of discrimination between animals qualified under the general regulations for admission will be exercised by the Chief of the Department of Live Stock, subject to the right of appeal to the Director General and National Commission.

The Illinois Woman's Exposition Board desires to learn whether it is permitted to solicit and receive from the women of Illinois, original applications for non-competitive exhibits, and to install the same, if approved, in the Illinois State Building, where space has been assigned for that purpose.

I should answer in the affirmative—that the Board has that right; not to conflict, however, with the rules and regulations which prescribe the character of the exhibits which are permitted in State buildings.

IOWA.—Will a great corn-producing State be permitted, in its State building, either as a decoration, an exhibit, or a restaurant, to serve the public in the best style of the culinary art with the great variety of forms in which maize may be prepared for human food?

No provision has been made for such privileges in State buildings.

Will the States be perm tted to use their discretion in supplying music at their respective State buildings during the continuance of the Exposition ?

Yes; subject to the general rules and regulations of the Exposition.

MASSACHUSETTS.—1. What duties does the President of the Board of Lady Managers desire the lady members of State boards to do ?

(Answered by Mrs. Potter Palmer, President of the Board of Lady Managers.)

Commissions coöperating with the Board of Lady Managers, will be asked to aid them:

1. To procure, for competition in the Main Buildings, a representative exhibit showing the work of women in all the varied occupations in which they engage.

2. To procure, as far as possible, statistics as to the amount of woman's work that enters into every exhibit, and other interesting data connected with the same.

3. To recommend to the Board work by women of such supreme excellence as to be worthy of admission to the gallery of the Woman's Building.

4. To recommend to the Board women who have the requisite expert knowledge to serve on various juries of award.

5. To see that the educational work, being carried on by women, from the primary to the highest branches of education, is exhibited when possible, and when not possible that it be illustrated by means of maps, charts, photographs, etc.

6. To see that the charitable and philanthropic work, as well as that to promote recreation, healthfulness, reform, etc., inaugurated by women, is either exhibited or made matter of record as above.

7. To aid in giving suitable publicity to the plans of the

Board of Lady Managers in all the leading papers, through the agency of press women, when possible.

8. To aid in collection of a loan exhibit of old lace, embroideries, fans, etc.

9. To secure the books written by women, for the Women's Library, especially such as relate to the exact sciences, philosophy, art, etc.

2. Shall the Executive Commissioners from each State correspond with the Chiefs of the different Departments, or must all correspondence relating to exhibits, pass through the office of the Director-General ?

The rule of the Board of Control on this subject is as follows:

All applications for space, and correspondence relating thereto, shall be addressed to the Director-General, who will cause an accurate record thereof to be kept in his office, and will direct the reference of such applications and correspondence to the Chief of that Department to which they properly belong, and thereafter the Chiefs of the respective Departments shall continue the correspondence with exhibitors, and shall supply blank applications for space in such form as the Director-General shall approve.

3. What are the desires of the Commission relating to the character of exhibits ? Are the State Commissions expected to reject offered exhibits, the purpose of which appears to be the use of the Exposition as a warehouse for the sale or advertisement of nostrums and decoctions, or shall the State Commission refusing those, be guided solely by a desire to place on exhibition only those products which shall best represent the development of science, brain, and skill ?

State Commission may advise, but can not decide finally upon the acceptance or rejection of any offered exhibit. It will be the policy of the management to exclude everything that is trifling or without value.

4. Is it the desire of the Chief of the Bureau of Liberal Arts, that each State shall at once take charge of the Educational ex-

hibit, and if so, will he furnish to each State at an early date a plan of the method which he has adopted for exhibiting same, giving to each State some idea of the space on which it can depend?

Dr. Peabody, the Chief of the Department of Liberal Arts, expects that some properly constituted authority in each State will collect, select, and forward the material for an Educational State exhibit. These exhibits will include all lines of Educational work supported at public cost and directed by public authority. An organized arrangement has been devised, in which the States will be separately placed, and at the same time, the different grades may be consecutively shown. The higher institutions will be grouped by themselves, in spaces included in the State allotments. Professional and technological specialties will be grouped together, to facilitate illustration and study. The allotment to the several States can not yet be made. The Chief seeks first to ascertain what States intend to exhibit, and what elements and institutions each will present.

5.   What action, if any, has been taken on the subject matter of the many petitions which our board has been informed have been sent to Chicago looking toward the erection of a separate building for the Department of Liberal Arts?

Petitions from Massachusetts and from other States have come to Chicago asking for a separate building for the Department of Liberal Arts. These petitions have been carefully considered. We have urged in every proper way the necessity of providing, if possible, a separate building for this Department; but we understand from the Board of Directors that it is not possible to erect a separate building for this purpose. We must carry out this Exposition on the lines already laid down. We have about 150 acres of floor space, and we must confine ourselves to that, and to our estimates of expenditure.

Some have asserted that we were going to give Education an insignificant place—to drive it into a corner. On the contrary, we assign to it a spacious place in the most magnificent building on the grounds. This great building has thirty-two acres on the ground floor, and with the second floor some forty acres for exhibits. The great Department of Liberal Arts will have about 400,000 feet of this space, amounting to over nine acres. It will occupy the entire south end of the building, opening on the main avenue of the Exposition. If we had the means to erect a separate building, I would prefer that, but the location assigned is central, ample, and worthy.

MISSOURI.—What manner of procedure will be adopted in entering our goods in the Woman's Building that will be satisfactory to both parties?

(Answer by Mrs. Potter Palmer, President of the Board of Lady Managers.)

The articles in the Woman's Building will be admitted by invitation, but State Boards are requested to report articles of superior excellence to the committee in charge of the installation of exhibits in that building.

NEW JERSEY.—1. How many exhibits of the same character showing the process of manufacture will be allowed?

This will be decided by the Chiefs of the respective Departments as the cases arise, subject to the approval of the Director General.

2. Will each exhibitor be allowed a concession for the sale of goods?

Every exhibitor may sell his goods or wares, using his exhibits as samples, and may deliver from a stock outside the Exposition. The articles exhibited may be sold for delivery after the Exposition closes, but (except perishable products) can not previously be removed.

For the sale of articles to be delivered on the grounds, a privilege or concession must be obtained, and special application must be made therefor, and the privilege or concession will be granted or withheld, at the discretion of the Ways and Means Committee.

3. Will exhibitors be allowed concessions for the sale of goods in more than one building?

This will be decided in accordance with the circumstances surrounding each case as it is presented. No general rule is provided.

4. Will any process of manufacture be allowed in buildings other than the Machinery Building to be operated by electric or other motors?

Probably not in the buildings of Manufactures and Liberal Arts, Fine Arts, Horticulture, and Fisheries; but processes will be allowed in the Machinery Department, and probably also in the Agricultural, Electrical, Mines and Mining, and possibly some other buildings.

5. Will power be furnished free of charge if exhibitor supplies motor?

A limited amount of power will be supplied free of charge; beyond that limit a moderate charge will be made.

The amount of power which will be supplied gratuitously and the price to be paid for extra power have not yet been decided.

6. How much power will be furnished as above?

Any amount of power reasonably required for the proper running of machinery, will be supplied on terms which will be stated when the permit for space is issued.

7. Will State boards be empowered to discriminate as to number of exhibits in any given class?

Their recommendation will have the consideration of the Chief of Department, but admissions or rejections will be primarily determined by the Chiefs of Departments, subject to the approval of the Director General, and with appeal to the National Committee, in case any proposing exhibitor whose application has been rejected claims the right to such appeal within reasonable time.

8. Will State boards also have power to accept or reject exhibits?

I should say not. The ultimate power of acceptance or rejection, is vested in the National Commission itself, as stated in the answer to question from Massachusetts. The recommendation of State boards will be respectfully considered, and we will organize in Philadelphia, New York, and other places, advisory boards to recommend exhibits. We have already such boards in the Department of Fine Arts. We will organize similar boards in other places for the acceptance of live stock, and for exhibits in other Departments, if desired. It will be necessary to have, in addition to the State boards, experts in many special lines to give us recommendations; but we will use the State boards and their committees in this way whenever they are willing to act.

NEW MEXICO.—Will exhibits from the various States and Territories be submitted to the local boards before acceptance by the Commission?

All domestic applications must be sent to the Director General, and it is immaterial whether they are sent direct by the intending exhibitor, or through his State or Territorial Board. The boards will, if they desire, be notified of all applications from their respective States or Territories, and can make such recommendations as they see fit regarding each application. These recommendations will be carefully considered, but final decision will rest with the National Commission.

Will the State and Territorial Boards have any authority in connection with the granting of concessions made to applicants of such States or Territories?

Their recommendations, whether favorable or unfavorable, would be considered by the Ways and Means Committee, and would have weight; but the Ways and Means Committee of the World's Columbian Exposition Company has the final power to reject any application for a concession. The power of acceptance is also vested in the same committee, subject to the approval of the National Commission.

Will concessions be made to more than one applicant from the same State or Territory for the sale of, or the manufacture and sale of, the same class of goods?

That is a matter to be decided by the Committee on Ways and Means, and can only be determined upon the merits of each case as it arises.

What commissions will be charged for concessions; what for the sale of articles manufactured and sold upon the grounds during the Exposition, and what for the sale of articles placed upon exhibition which are sold to be delivered at the close of the Exposition?

The percentage of royalty or amount of bonus to be charged for any concession will be determined by the Ways and Means Committee on each case as it arises, and the same rule will apply to privileges for the sale of goods manufactured on the grounds.

No commission will be charged, or restrictions placed, upon the sale of exhibits for delivery after the close of the Exposition, or of articles sold by sample and delivered outside of the Exposition.

Arrangements for the sale of perishable exhibits may be made with the Chiefs of the several Departments, under regulations prescribed by the Ways and Means Committee.

If exhibits are accepted by the local State Board, will they be put upon exhibition, provided they can be placed within the allotted space?

They will be put upon exhibition if they are accepted by the Chief of the proper Department. No article of any kind, or from any source, should be shipped to Chicago for exhibition until a permit for space, signed by the Director General, is in the hands of the person who made the application for space.

When will the allotment of space in the several Departments be made?

We hope to have allotments of space for domestic exhibits made by next July, probably not before.

Will there be an allotment of space to the various States and

Territories to be occupied by persons from such States and Territories desiring concessions ?

There will be no general allotment of space for concessions,
but each application for a concession will be considered by
itself on its own merits, and if granted, the grant will carry with
it the space necessary for conducting the business.

RHODE ISLAND.—Can anyone whose application for space has
been rejected by the Commission of his own State, secure consideration from the Board of Reference and Control for such rejected
exhibits?

State Boards will not be given the authority to accept or
reject exhibits. The final decision will rest with the Commission,
through its Board of Control, or its executive officer, the Director
General. An unfavorable report on an application made to any
State or Territorial Commission would, however, go very far in
influencing action, but a rejected applicant can not be deprived
of the right of appeal.

TENNESSEE.— Has any arrangement been made with railroads
for transportation of material for State buildings and State
exhibits, and upon what terms?

The Traffic Department is at work, and has made an arrangement under which all domestic exhibits can be brought here at
one fare and returned free. It is endeavoring to get additional
concessions from the several railroads. I do not understand that
any special arrangements are yet made for building material. I
think that is left to the several States.

WISCONSIN.—In the blank applications for space it is stated
that the exact space each article will take up must be given. In
many cases this is impossible. Will it then be sufficient for the applicant to state the number of square feet, or the length and width
of space, required for applicant's display of goods, without giving
exact space to be required by each specific article proposed to be
displayed?

The total space required in square feet should be given. An exhibitor may send an application for four or five different articles, but he must give a drawing to the scale of one-fourth inch to the foot, showing the general location of the articles he proposes to exhibit.